THEATRICS

JOHN CROUSE

mOnocle-Lash Anti-Press

2024

Previous Publications

Belows	2001, Broken Boulder Press, Santa Monica (cover by Stanley Zappa)
Hunkers	2001, Xtantbooks, Charlottesville
Conscripts	2003, Book & CD by Stanley Zappa, Portland; performed at Disjecta in Portland Or, Feb 27, 2003
Speechings	2005, Xpressed, Finland (cover by Stanley Zappa)
Constitutes	2007, Effing Press, Austin (published in a flipchap w/ Obstructs, a prose text.)
Universes	2011, Differentia Press, Santa Maria
Says	2023, Litmus Records, Finland (Music by Jukka-Pekka Kervinen)

Theatrics, by John Crouse

ISBN 978-1-948637-10-7

mOnocle-Lash Anti-Press

Cover Image © Brian Counihan

Cover Design by Olchar E. Lindsann

BELOWS

Act One, Chapter One

Voice

Apparently at age zero set the clocks rewound broke harmony measures twice. Stay your loose ends all trigger fingers raining cool to read it by that window like you then you could pull it out. Do it good & it's something old, but only a minute old. Greatest of the greatest mouthfuls of places.

Voice

Books a treasure, a rehash become absolute.

Voice

Terminal mystic trues your machine for it to come off as speech. Paley strike yourself slimmer for banging belly-up dark belows. Unwebbed at crashed skin from bone by skin but stuck grin sweating ellipsis booty upends urns and sifts through.

Voice

Knucklehead with rodent climbing. Getting wet to booked as trotted nuns tits hands flail to belong to. Gave limelight a startle. Typical, it's had all its startles.

Voice

Dross epic vomits external heart watermark dungs when wholeness falls apart as a value. Hello, country bumpkin. Who information? Polyseme? Have it be that short life. Remember me after dismember me. Rewind for your especially boss crotch novel.

Act One, Chapter Two

Voice

Cream jugs hence your headlines. Joy boy joy jelly joy knob. Guarded out, grew another limb of got half again bigger. Sorts seemed to have sorted, having had a real zest it. As clouds move, move shades on the ferns. Dry-humping leaves, banyon & cloister.

Voice

Be, a tentacle toward immediate day after & by the second. In, after & burying peanuts in sizable domains, say it isn't true, but be. Have it down so mesh is made flesh is your same weave.

Voice

How many times the window frame? Fan a sky a tree crest, a roof, Venus, at night. Sleeping below your kiss and tit fuck day such as screamer harborside orchestral strolled colored senses passageway heart eight. Yesterdays of flowers rides of flowers. Headword typeface cheese girl picking along then flows gushes.

Voice

Perspective meditate cycles drafts circling chopped data a trillion. Blue sky melts pattycake melts an aqua jolts gentle seeping data. Perfect ground above a river clouds could storm.

Voice

Tread on green flowers, tiger that knows oceans better by albatrossing.

Act One, Chapter Three

Voice

Where doors open fluid shadows catch stomps. At once prance one more a fluid shadow snatches a moment's gain. Capture of the capture to that moment's the same as. Caught at deeping before daylight, flitting the open every door, jerking wrestles trees & coups & stars caught as whip or whatever taken like wow.

Voice

Something possible to ape man done grunted a frank of prose. Where's the narrative questions throughout? Form-wise w/ tinkering narrative notes. Dances on it kicked wholes through stinking its blowhole. Guess who you are. Friends fag the isotopes. Not to sense past to tinue, how to keep pissing out the window bites & tastes of living? Windy circular routes blow rain lashes down grates as murken bone through skin of water oddly. Undulating mass accomplished into steam.

Voice

Conjure it up to semblance your soaking dream about the pain, see all about its ten or eleven drips inching to the sky, a dozen stitches not matching perfect the grey shroud, & jays, blue dogs in their carpet burn satchels lurking where their banging is, swing crowy as maces in the trees as though that it's a fragile situation is no secret.

Voice

Yikes, groove, eke, bloody nose, my only sole bout to come, new, mush the pound, my groovy patters!

Act One, Chapter Four

Voice

Something's endless used to be earlier than now. Dear resonance's raspings are continually hisses. Wobbling head reeling happy whole gut. Water w/ intent to breathe season stretched as razored hash. Notice of yellow groove you white. What's not in the not really there sea drain?

Voice

Do not come at me with your school. Wake up. Let's go look at the tree of life. Where is that? Just have bad timing. It's fun. It's miserable. Three months to get outside October. Guts where chests hunch waver jives at suck off. Tacked rendering hymned virgin makes them see dancing suns in Spain.

Voice

Educate at firm cock.

Voice

Dutch boy or windblown? Ray gun alchemist crackles at moment's schmaltz some butterflies a couple odes kilter. Quick, paint something pretty in an airless room.

Voice

When he comes out his tummy is going to explode into a rocket kept breathing more impermanent than a perfect bound event.

Act One, Chapter Five

Voice

Kooking cheap wheeler spiels reportage but a belly punch seeps. Memorize the sun's out. Don't force it. Time don't tell pow puckering the extra inch oft uncramps it. Pin what down?

Voice

Jutting tits minds polish on par with cosmos. Have great laughter. What's the clock? Still throw their nights yet? That's a far far something pain away from. Never don't be, speed. Would you adorn me with goo? She's on page forty-two. It comes along every now and then to redeem.

Voice

Whatever yo do that pools like gravity make me not cross my legs like chicken tendon from the same category of finding the best way of torturing with a squirt bottle is just like cat balls into possum. Look, this that's called adjustment is deep deepa deep deep, rubberband, rubberband man. Make me not cross my legs! Thinking about capillaries cartel is in your nose like tendon, which is from the same category, larvae more distinct.

Voice

Let, let an ocean fall! Fall down! To its night sets in a west & tar, tar logs beach the mother pounds!

Act One, Chapter Six

Voice

Boom! Take a whiff. There's your childhood. Remember the dance. Don't let the day die. Fifteen drunk the skeleton. Who needs to make him scary? Bye, birdy, first great extremity. So, old was right up to see a blah line telling away from fulls felt close & quiet washed still to gleam?

Voice

Such bliss at seeing do oops at screaming. Bigging yikes fountain stride breaths. See? You don't like it, do you? You're reading fast oils. Beyond what suffering the whole game halves? Some whatnot depending resolute must've been moron bending backwards. Floating have calm energy. Plunk one's twanger. Big breasts do it good. Smiles wait till she's started, telling drop.

Voice

See even what wells exact moment busses pass you back & shoot away from, say cheese, tacky shotput heaved, one of many. What about abeyance for belie, this once? Leisure is a gift to bob for. Even given what you could take of grips outdoors harking shudders nonstop the matters how it drips. Plug the corn bin. Shit, hippy, you're cracking.

Voice

Spikes louve, sneak, blooden my lung bone white, my soul comes, ooh, rush, the sound, knotty boobies, slapper!

Voice

Word erected shit in a can toyed atrocities voiced missives stepped in hoppy shop carnage. Jacked plenty all forms. Canvas though cloaking one & only unforeseen. Is nothing there?

Act One, Chapter Seven

Voice

Belly button the seesaw point of the moon says nothing as canon says nothing, oh, bitingly, so don't be giving it that sound to inflation, nothing to actual. Dismemberment were repetition were devoted shrine. That comments nothing, save whipped to peevish asshole-cashed perpetuation of woe frictioning your all-more gained mandating suppers at history's font vomiting department store candor.

Voice

Let's go bald on top but still have ponytails. Enter clean cloud body shines budging traces turning attached air knowledge to headlines to visual bloated tummy tots stroking typeface abstracts. Nordstrom memories mean more family time. Trick or treatise?

Voice

Blind geek to pie tin. Come in, pie tin. Meat eater power? Onion powder. Gallivant, gammo, gank.

Voice

Give us a P! Give us an L! Give us an O! Give us a T! Each instance of this & this newfound breath to exterior moves.

Voice

Give me a break. Dig October's last day, batteries not included.

Act One, Chapter Eight

Voice

Minivan parades whores thighs chested, jeepers. I forgot my milk money. So, mow & cut, look at his beer gut, look at your dusk. Stopping a hills flows arches winter-naked skeleton cycles images cleaves wheeling. Skyline! Meditate the lines. Waggle your fixture spins for substance. Fakes your nerves. Triphthong.

Voice

Dimension, square, white. Pick as separate feather hairs stand out, speaking as gulls flap alleys, their routes semantics. Or is it that its anon stinky sock named hanging a bum cinching his growing gut's butt food?

Voice

Drinking blue paint, everything was body as prize at dark coming on glade trees & light went through. Body as much a tree to house and be, lot's a lot, take it from anywhere being done. Sunlight quickly is. Sky gives trees blue motions.

Voice

Geek to digress, yet remove the tree, remove it from the forest. It then it's dead.

Act One, Chapter Nine

Voice

To the ham hammer, to the saw sawing, run away, run awaymering with cache of poems before the woods are gone. Flesh brokers biscuit hooks. Either or. Bookmark of gorillas. It's just junk. Let's go to sleep in a park. Let's fuck. Tenuous. You remember that one. Like a sea breeze & open windows on busses piss mouth-breathers off. Who's springing for force-fed lungs?

Voice

Hi, scenic. How'd you get so? Whew, heating up forn the sun. Graveyard strips down limbs. Time to change the tamp. After a big storm, sure there are limbs down. Frigger, globular beater. Wouldn't grinding it skeleton bad planetary configuration? Vows for daily living, in verse. Chrono apes that slush blue from plastic, cheeses a dimple or something real candy.

Voice

Go in amazement, fucker. Twenty-one slats, a growling barrage there, white. Clouds are bigger than the moon. Swap ya a sore neck for a gold warbler.

Voice

Raw Wanda. Daily true green red fast Uganda jam.

Act One, Chapter Ten

Voice

To every coherent sheaf assign elements of your pivoting caper. Emergent pupa, bobbing, sparkles a way to earth songs' daft superstructures auditioning for elastic deflection mod roles of rupture. Exist at corners. Duce a blenden fect.

Voice

Waterline sentences each always death. Spacer blocks little buddy, the fuck-up, stacks stacks on your rudder room.

Voice

Nodal load pattywhack blakes the mack as interior of your eye boots its stem. Some like their duck cooked rarer than most. Brainstem toasts array of elements of elements of elements frothing basal hyperstatic riff, give a dog a bone.

Voice

Total dimensions support sweet scene. Single points of view porn loop styles at terminal cluster, eggs standing at equinox. Universe's galaxies are bigger, but not in mass. A blast!

Act One, Chapter Eleven

Voice

Nut-less heels fractures all static considered deformations grazed toward a going to be just pixie dust. Complex. Loading patterns unscribble all repivoted on the whisker. Boa hackles slightest feather from a little ostrich hurl kills best on warm days linear strand doses. Ships rain spacesuits walking spillways start & why not, if in going, why shouldn't you be looking to take some down with? The top of your love slinking the top of the morning thinking the top of your tits bringing the top of your gob surging the top of your lungs rolling atop of the grass fucking.

Voice

Chopping data, level head collects wafts openploded jackly. Mostly in foliage. Bramblethick wend breath each stifling exclaim. So wend so. Suggest notion slaps? Details stagger spray can raptures squall gold slopes. Everywhere death is pores opening or not.

Voice

Heard choppy blocky with smooth edges makes a good fuck. Nothing doing with long lost anything resounding unknown assess staking stalks toward empty spaces, same torsos away filling panic with sure smiles.

Voice

Collage taught stares at your crotch bitched smiles about. Like what tits do for hundreds of bucks? Pent air wrings brains over a living there's landing gear. Black it. Seen pure mind's good pride?

Act One, Chapter Twelve

Voice

Dutched smogs happy yet rumor crinkling the foil of would have done is sun castrated, world looking sitting on horns swiped mudmold breasts from a ledge snowflake. As tumble by deflate is what's to stop not fall rather glide.

Voice

Buoyant then fashion of jag chocolating colors is what's to stop without a best part of pissing in closed book seal prewrite cock-less enough to peal erect charm gone chime wenting to gulp spices wherein all exhales are fathomed, slapping leaves the way around.

Voice

The face fell down into the meat. Clear mind soaking sun's pristine soot likewise cloaks crammed pearls of air drafts dirging dallying fuckflights fumbling touches at reveries' tip. Throat straps alive compared to rocking horse in strobe-lit tomb.

Voice

Silver tears mean sadness? Have great laughter. You might get the cookie chute. Add trickest cornball oddity fouled Velma's panties. Emergency room treatment amounting to admin of spit cup. Pray your higher authority's hung himself.

Act One, Chapter Thirteen

Voice

Route etch big smile being Pacific woods' wet-grey, morning fuck for grinding grove right in day. Rumble does hunger again castrated to quench, rubbing shoulders clanged by spitted hands put back black bras in drawers. Ream stays intact glides a-keel from demise this needle hopes to dye walks of the hour flurrykicking hymns to calm.

Voice

Powder horn humping leapfrog cheeks your filling gulp today futured. Only grey pregnates windowturns away next day to next day bet your ass damn straight I would blacken. Says who? Wonderland drizzles bed comedies. Why not the eight head? Lid see cherry red pucked her face bossed gladdening her calm head.

Voice

Deem it the wisest of rapes to have thought you without fail would repeel the fallenbeard mossy stump's banana hole each time but wet leaves, you say, keep it tidy. To have thought you could binocular the thing and that you would stay there, in place, imagining what the hardon is about, wherever it is, and formally spit at the cop's torso bulging acetylene at your sexy kryptonite necklace. Better roots than thighs, those roots snake. Could be you smile when you wad as liquids are not artifact until they dry, who cares? You damn sure will when another's boot prints the orchard, then the whole son of a bitch will stop working, mark said avatar DNA will hereby coagulate, jellied backlog, daisy chain brittling to birdseed vultures taboo, glove the cornpone.

Voice

Boo, I like the move my body speaks, ram home pole, came, mush the mound, sprained wrists at the staid fatter!

Act One, Chapter Fourteen

Voice

Big deal, calling the whyfor of falling objects gravity whams pantywaisted, g for god, easy grind, whispers reckoning splintering collisions animal magnetism though dodo's the fowl's tag, duh, d for dog or for whomever hands it out.

Voice

Dawnblue skies not one nowhere near as fizzing out as this or any sentence, an ass braying & quaking its state & meaning as soon meant, unpinnable. Roundstick finelines so what tangents innumerable smiles pending a whichway come at, enabled flypaper girded slickjelly as per come all fracas in the fall.

Voice

Somewhere immediately throat clicks. Propped that tooting peel sunny how DNA is in ejaculate, can't stop. What drives this thing? Keys or chains in hand as scoop shoveling poem. Rhyme interrupted spirals opening though and opened scattering fog lights swerves.

Voice

More a millions now, floating & telling mesh, hey mesh, your canyon's only seething. Iron lung to your right. Animal an end to itself anything is? Upstairs might move if a wind shakes.

Voice

What's culled of frictions by meted supposed fractions this day scribedraughts onward as dispositions shouting solid imposes at the seen head forefronting doggedly agile black pane's illumed traces. Making words by way of explanation, end quote.

Act One, Chapter Fifteen

Voice

Certainty leisures in a three zombie super tub by crooked resource afloat on long-maligned logarithm's sea, stinkers monikered sporty for cappers. Bogus proponents expound matters of dust lighting, zingers ringered matter of course.

Voice

The sailing, spoke, heard & seen nothing of mass grave mistakes, gene structure oopsies let to mark swirldown as fleeting instances, go fish. Stooges deem offhand your final void as drowning straight flush, spunquick components carved in such cured wood.

Voice

Say, as if it's solely what to know, that if the skein shivering unraveled hives in you then it buzzes us all, that your gimped idiotcards stack the deck, that perpetuity's blindered, what, go ahead, no one's listening. Sore your own neck, your breath smokes, real prophetic. Turn again, stow us the other hide, secular coat, matter of rhyme. Time, as you're apt, your bides, & ply that seamless gaze close to bark, go on, cool seared grain by bowlegged hornstomps fit to roust niggard mole, ninny's events, om gonna de fine yer per am eaters, give you vague in a sweet basket, meantime, your bummer jackass doubtless is for booting.

Voice

Out of sights, so, I is a freak, my tongue won't bite, butter roll, dark nights, come again, hawhaw, whew, gain flush the round, creamy corner!

Voice

Every bar's ballet music, strains & whiffs as structures grabs, grappled handfuls of commas walking tenderly to the commode. Did it shock you? Look what I bite off. See a way a day happens.

Act One, Chapter Sixteen

Voice

Conjuring the more of purging chant spells motions besides flows out heaps tossing a sky's color. Tell knowing out of lines a can be exploding past revel freedom hunghuge a depressed four-sheeted tom-tom may be open may curve. Light falls a wing's hatches.

Voice

Sail, far as the reef of mangled hulls, toothpick atoll. One's company where there's personality disorder wrested from what don't compute balmed into broke sextants lenses dry-heaving at Venus like fantasy & Santa Claus for consolation.

Voice

Gift horse was gimped when you got him. Usage panel? Pervert peanut butters preschool apples, campy splucks mostly get it off then let it go rancid. What is maintained? Why? Tongues stuck for good. Lockjawed face she turns to singing birth. Inexplicable. Fixed depth rooting of the same causeway to busted record recitation of ventriloquist vows.

Voice

A plus them lip smacks. Unison stabbed don't matter. Archives the place? Clenched design spells it meantime. Counterfeit teleology wilts pickup sticks. Smell how scared. Ape money pious to qualify in the testicular time trial. Witch doctor says pinto beans.

Act One, Chapter Seventeen

Voice

Bare-titted ghost smooth talks molecular renounce of curves' endless bounces by bending elbows jacking tears in the blue. Knifed wide neon slushing at dawn's open mouth falling gone & going black. Whole deadening of the cock's calling screaming hails off trees.

Voice

So conflated, the body, stuffed by vacuum, throws no shadows in noon light. Blue to ball harsh dormancy stone sobriety sinks or swims in step with walking death.

Voice

Repent to a point prescribed? Upper lip at gaunch, lower at skysack pulled when the snakes start yapping. Soundingboard purveys collective limps be walking planks on hips. Passion play toots songs of pureskin praises. Baby butt loots your convoluted crotch leaf fictions blank.

Voice

Screw the sentence. Resonant enchanter vibes Oh skipper I dig your goatee. Lull me and glaze me noodled! Chart tacks cobalt sky to it. Airbrush dupe you? Fart textures tension chiseled in dayglo tumblewad rivulets precoordinated by yokels, trite pee flacciding to crabby bunk wherewas pristine whores' beds. Lapses halt longings. Jog the infinite committed sacrilege spree! Remedial blows can be turned down if each must suffer these same bad metaphors.

Act One, Chapter Eighteen

Voice

I plan to net you in my ribcage as sky is my tunnel there. Is it because one instant ago I remembered you? Now the instant's forever. What's the difference? Who forgets something hard in their pocket? Move back the last bagging day. Jimmy the stone because the sky is big, the calendar fat.

Voice

It had to give, was that it? What gives? Something did, something about a sundial. Certainly the sky's ripping. Whose fault's that? Cunt hairs dipped in hum soft parts. Remedial breathing hurts how much? Thunderous missives out mixing gold faucet spins the just add water to poetry's mud. Dismal grounding, drown the world. New kind of flashy.

Voice

Fuck that noise. What's got your feet treading's got you only dreaming you're climbing out a splendid sea chest of gold oxygen & freshest treasure. Settle on a nice pair of anything. Fuck the autopilot. Pallbearer take you there. Simply subtract you from the world's weight in flesh.

Voice

Suck, if looks could, then your face just swallowed bobbing umpteen ways of doing the fish mouth. Stick to that chippy nee nippy half way past the sun. No book yet knows the half that's swallowed after enough heat?

Act One, Chapter Nineteen

Voice

You will not again tie my tongue for frozen it was swallowed, action promising, for its part, to shall speak in at least air whispers trickles sweet drool. Not no vacancy but treading death on uneven plastic limbs of terminal removal detain your natural order willing rape codifies. It's as though one's head and not fresh air is moisture's house, immediate map after the build-up.

Voice

Howls dodging the ass press canted damp frowns against the eel and into the cloud-housed flintwheel, one bitten it own ass rolling unpresumptive already at a sea's parched start, the other cranking heights of ructioning air.

Voice

Such a deal, cracking tight pussy at sloped blue oblivion one needn't wager caution, fee simple, airborne skyscrapers. No more stucco, concrete, or siding? Listen to how boulders lichen & deer rut. Hung wisping at breast a twiddling & curdy batter with seam for clenching. Pavlov spikes at the cuddle grown on you?

Voice

Audible rebar washes zenith of yelled dozes. Diaper changes at thirty thousand feet. Never mind the adult genitals, they are poeming. Full-size beam bumps to glide intact on. Rethread your revel at the sensually dying part. Teethe at memory's start. Slow panting soak of the first ware stretches back sheer to shake rattle.

Act One, Chapter Twenty

Voice

Did it shock you? Remembered light grooves head rolled into a center. Respirating cruxes scratch shapes. Lurching footing pumping blood breaks speaking move at blocking necks. Glimpse hapless glimpse skyline. Dot-dashing enough?

Voice

Objective acrobatted, flipping and bulged out the middles your squalid percolate. Seething nearly tocketing skeleton pocks a millions limbs of dead man skin as leaves lace the whole jerky coming roared. Loping faultless so elegant so far.

Voice

Bitchin. Trick is, dipping pole in lurkwater, to spy the rawhide outsides where chaff physics feet per second on the same priceless chart goatropers ply this and that ruse. Dipped in what? Vaginas cakewalk casket into a world's secret time and place mobs, tuck, what's that smell? Strutted brainjugs dropjaw at hilarious screw you.

Voice

A queen her hymen, a queen her chocolate tiara, a queen her girlhood, absences rain reveals. Rock and roll, you gasping and holy tot, your dream, hello, for its smell, is gone.

Voice

It was a sparkle laying here that it was a secret that I could make that.

HUNKERS

Scene One

Me

Watched corpse and got off on your rump again.

You

Place to be as your body must come along so too your brain.

Me

There's the manure spreader.

You

Shot your load, which see, vitally on red meat.

Me

Breathe out and lungs empty.

You

Sort of a big muscle.

Me

Self-speaking flow rather dickly keeping an attitude spinning.

You

Poems of what happens?

Scene Two

Me

Don't lose your rights colliding your clock plain view.

You

Escape tones much less individuality.

Me

Play face how ever the shapes differ.

You

Vicarious rape calms culture yourself sexy.

Me

Open casket bad cops stand on felled loose lippings cunt.

You

You must be the earth dancing flower.

Me

Hard hobbit honor.

You

Have it be urgent.

Scene Three

Me

Fuck all this stuff of breaths.

You

The place where the inhaling breath is born, my ass.

Me

Nourishing lovebirds, more like it.

You

More ilk than the same.

Me

From moment to moment the tree explains itself?

You

Before the needles threaded turned to be ice.

Me

Take a bite.

You

Hunkers prose through blank verse playing cards on a toilet.

Scene Four

Me

You like bubble first?

You

Paint a cage with an open door.

Me

Revert, launch your everywhere really works.

You

Quick, stool the most obvious dance that after three coffees happens.

Me

Tell what's true.

You

Testicles didn't pinpoint, did help locate.

Me

In changes wanting to convolute all it said.

You

A strange thing loved from dying damaged very deep.

Scene Five

Me

Is there a difference?

You

Conventional chest are all people.

Me

Personal once upons want balls snuggled at double loop ripe breasts.

You

Recharge different.

Me

Rooms in a motherfucking crater.

You

Freud's cunt.

Me

Loom farthling some must be undercouch cushions worth past.

You

Jackal pretense as tow truck clanks opera nights.

Scene Six

Me

You have to talk in language who will understand?

You

Ideally no repetition as you walk by in your panties.

Me

Kongo-inflected black tomb.

You

You thing the turban scared them?

Me

Grazing thighs before battle signs deathed solar winds blown from the sun.

You

Stars viewed from space are little little do not twinkle.

Me

Most cases takes just a single noose to cinch it.

You

Knockers is a word is a word is a world.

Scene Seven

Me

Is the genital unhampering free?

You

A third step in refining a mind is eat shit & die.

Me

At scoops clip this earnest despite thinking there's anything.

You

Anything itself as broad as no things white rose no knocks.

Me

See what sounds your prototype keen eye archives, big daddy, at mote's crank.

You

Make a world taste good.

Me

Jack it free from diction aka drop the underpants, underpass queen.

You

Do watch the bust laid when jack to the drawing board's exactly a sermon.

Scene Eight

Me

Fluctuate the punctuate, suck the puncture?

You

Probably heart of you surprised the heart of me.

Me

Can lark stuff the apprenticeship essay down your throat?

You

Is there no duplication?

Me

Help you to find the proper luster?

You

Words as ideas naming perversion cocks your default cone.

Me

Crap it already.

You

Spent half the crapper on the morning poeming.

Scene Nine

Me

Afterfuck trails thru whitewoods as purple smallest face mounts icy stairs up the dark.

You

To today glown how innocence contours hills, throws trees out stark?

Me

Skreeking hammock wound oiled at the ass ends frictions to lick your snowstuck make-do.

You

How many toadstools do you count?

Me

Your hero's slooped on all fours.

You

Who won best actor?

Me

Pencil strapped to your member inklings brokedick chickenfoot draggings reamed.

You

Limply uncontrolled writhing kept up could write tomes.

Scene Ten

Me

Time marked & filed in surplus cabinets, do what?

You

Quick studies prior to flushing.

Me

Good reads.

You

Current events downriver.

Me

Fiction life's stuffed of arresting freedom to body's expressions at your sources.

You

Floated & stared at the sun moving lips into sleeping verbs after the ass piece.

Me

Coherency an attempt to still chattered touchbottom efforts to reconcile.

You

Where's the fucking?

Scene Eleven

Me

Your praiseworthy doper suddenly realizes whisks is why.

You

Caps at carry your pounded out deep ruts save it for drymouth blue sunday afternoons.

Me

Those heavens among grips.

You

Pureray stomp juice from a chalice almost tears on you.

Me

Don’t choke on the sunset.

You

Unbosom your heart now.

Me

Wobble always here you is enough.

You

You want me to tell you all the people who love you?

Scene Twelve

Me

Cock-fought donut it piss you off?

You

Slug witty meatstraw tantrum emcee cow but a bitch hefted as dipped or four-hooved.

Me

Pining to be jacked?

You

Make forefinger & thumb all sacral & face happy, sad, juicy?

Me

What wonderful as a poem, what wonderful big knockers.

You

Squirtying mouths, guards kept down.

Me

Lowest river stopped twas get your head out your ass.

You

Stylistic invention, give me a break.

Scene Thirteen

Me

More like stifle stifle stifle de-lifed we breathing de-lifed breathed life the moment's chafe.

You

Moron three thousand languages worldwide.

Me

Bigshot formality found airless re-found hot monoxide.

You

Three thousand course study certificates of first lingos furred & smelling like wet pussy.

Me

Enchilada dab & mop electroshock cold blue secrets handkerchiefed.

You

Better to frame & fistfuck & hand one hairy emeritus.

Me

Order & everything in its time.

You

Go to the heart person, itself shitting buddhas.

Scene Fourteen

Me

Did you say that to hurt me?

You

It causes like a backwash thru your heart.

Me

Fashionable word stacks.

You

You're wearing about four layers.

Me

Let's get some air circulating.

You

Guess who deems what goes?

Me

Scream convulsions madder to write home about.

You

Pulse & clamor of pleads & implores dins your death rattle.

Scene Fifteen

Me

Living death inch-long nipples the snake mud-splats.

You

Will she blow your cover?

Me

Former ways linger fit to reprint your cherished classic stand the test of time's emptying lick.

You

Brutal orgasm repairs stacked skins ripe upon instinct.

Me

Big-ass gush of wadshots filling your head translates as voodoowand swizzling.

You

Stop the world, you've stubbed your toe?

Me

Good for churning milk seas on your back called butter.

You

Link it shall hinder love to freedom to genuine mental candy.

Scene Sixteen

Me

Cosmic lightning strike at your etcetera tolled your story's omissions.

You

As linear within line heard loudness grinding cessation's sky-high lollipop.

Me

Present asshole puckers knew who you were.

You

Kind of shit where the bastard comes a close grip fuck it.

Me

Hair pulled over periods?

You

Hear the loudness.

Me

Couldn't it be boss had there were notten parenthesis?

You

Where is the subtlety & then where's the why the sissy craft at drumming any what?

Scene Seventeen

Me

Bludgeon icepickingly exact flesh bone soul in the exactful.

You

So that storm oceans lull storms the awe fucking to so bold new words for yearning?

Me

Dunes spent senses unseen to then inward dunes fill booming seams.

You

Are you the earth-dancing flower?

Me

Where is the tension collision repair?

You

Santa hat is a bunch of shit.

Me

Do the lip purse where you know you have equidistant tipis creaming bullets.

You

Something really dug a lot of sucking something.

Scene Eighteen

Me

Living's motions the perfect art.

You

Dovetailed shit-for-brains be blowing me something scrumptious man, amen.

Me

Grew another limb of got half-again bigger.

You

Sorts seemed to have sort has a real zest it.

Me

You've nice things hanging there.

You

Hollywood cancan lets you concentrate on pudding words together or taking them apart.

Me

Dickbone's connected to the.

You

The truest attendance, always.

Scene Nineteen

Me

Your butthole's shot your butthole's shot whose poopoo?

You

Write a sunshaft and watch the money roll in.

Me

Workplace hope.

You

Through the sky's a perception.

Me

Your rote book on a platter gushes hotly coming numerical gushes.

You

Narrative withers?

Me

Win a heart, sugar an avenue as well as ink strangled references.

You

Consider as myth corporate porn fuck.

Scene Twenty

Me

Turns out you suck.

You

Last rustle at night compares to sheets to the wind.

Me

In the boxcar there is no need to kiss anyone's ass or china teacup.

You

Which underwear are clean?

Me

Do your manicure first.

You

Process told by rigged narrator stories written running water.

Me

Did you sugar me timber?

You

O what a lovely pussy you have, scat!

CONSCRIPTS

Act Zero

"Somebody Heard Mercurial Bump"

"Which Iffy Is This One Called?"

"Its The One With Top Pain"

"Numberless Living Editions Clemency Uneven Oracle"

"Expels Living Space"

"Cartoon Worry Disjoints Braggarts To Strike Blossoms Turgid"

"Welcome To Opportunity Charms"

"This Coalesce Might Be A Good One"

"Moot Upper Face Ornate Is Called Heedlessly"

"Sequences Detached Aims Peril Along Sorrows Length"

"Over Series Flows Dilated Portable Distances Threnodys Directions"

"Be There In A Jiffy"

Act One

"Habits Of Freeing Strengthen Baubles Sensations Chorus"

"Banned Social Flathead Determines Supernatural"

"Unsteady Packs Lacks Composure Unlocks"

"Looting Recreation Reigns Continuity Beaches"

"Question Marks Suffering From"

"Prefaces That Scooting Meander Rolls Unfinished"

"Ruins States Of Attracts Over Sayings Divine"

"Purpose Delight Dramas Splices Plus A Crisis"

"Job Fair Skeletons Mouthfeel Formats Link Jungle Gym Tizzies"

"Lips Corrective Pelvis Simian Folds Zombie Essays Jitterbugged"

"Meteors Mock Warhead Goons Composition Brambles"

"Folklore Into Coughing Buckshot Soundalikes Quagmire"

Act Two

"Kid Rocker Pointyheads Graffiti Mister Coffee Destabilizes"

"Commodity Horizon Falses Atmospheres Languages Rule"

"Jellyfish Foodscraps Self Worth"

"Break The Tense Connecting Flow"

"Obstructs Prefaces Scenario Tinkers Books Evolves"

"Tentacles Toxin Straightjacket Tickles"

"Heavens Visited To Music Rising Swerves Nucleus"

"Act To Chapters Indentures Apes For Jamming Readymades"

"Modes Latrine Decrees To Dark Workshop Analysis"

"Rolldown Repulsion Fetches Continuum Tallies Schemes"

"Marketplace Wisdom Roller Derby Stenches Utters Colossal"

"Baubles Fall Grand Designs Blank Spaces Composite"

Act Three

"Tend Memory Dullness"

"Growing Motion Novelties Discourse Obliges Piecemeal Overlap"

"Precious Codes Phantom Syllabi Sidewinder"

"Deforming Genuflecting Passions Constitutions Passions Episodes"

"Bigger Specks Game Universe As One Freedom Merges"

"As Goals Isolate Thirst Cycles Bosoms Unscribbled"

"Graces Scrambler Past Senses Scuttlebutt Bamboozles Breath Streams"

"Spry That Withered Erection As Bonbon Cultures Agency"

"Motionless To Frazzle"

"Cognition Honey Showmanship Pitches Tents Blockheads Sestets"

"Resolutions Spell Out Books Offshoots Idiot Box Headdresses"

"Jeering Turbulence Particularly Epistles Torture Breaking Into Sonnets"

Act Four

"Barbed Wire Incantations Cahoots Deflower"

"Tuning To Soundings Parentheticals Onwards Entrances"

"Spells Books Unbound"

"Afterlife Honky Scatterloads Airspace Inklings"

"Homemade Parade Obliterates Ample Dazzles Epistles"

"Heffalump Aqualung Climaxes Humming Books Sounds"

"Megastar Crackhead Ciphers Quakes A Human Shield"

"Air Crystals Birds"

"Pay Per View Primal Roam Morphs Rebuttals Monkey Glands"

"Thermonuclear Tracksuit Miniscules Icebergs"

"Rations Angry Young Mans Shoeshine Traumas"

"As Gas Chamber Meat Lozenges"

Act Five

"Slippery Skeletons Flip Flopping Deckhand Talent Cock"

"Parenthesis For Tracheotomy Blames"

"Dixie Cup Wishlist Went Ahead & Woodchipper"

"Genitals Quotidian Harmonys Aims"

"The Plays The Thing"

"The Serious Catch All"

"No Citing Influences"

"Thats No Name Tag"

"Let Talking Spill Out Harnessed Forms"

"Demeaning Scrutinys Prick Overwhelms Past Guessings"

"Comfort Constricting Flipsides"

"Pinpricking Nectars Syringes"

Act Six

"Endless Cradle To Wasted Sunset"

"Classifications Dusk Continuing Blue Sky"

"Golden Places Are Propped Any Traces"

"Electric Alcohol Manatee Achieves Novelty"

"Crusader Verse Can Be Roars Stock Devices"

"Wrought Per Formed Sublime Yoke Preaches"

"Stay Like That For A Few Minutes"

"Recurring Spoken Chapters Folktale Conscripts Merge"

"Spectators Cloudseeding Broke Into Song"

"Rising Lumps Of Air Freshen A Great Veil"

"There Occasionally Is A Halo"

"Masterpiece Endorses Overlapping Dissolves Tabulated"

Act Seven

"Devout Shitcan Mutterings Transcript Red Carpet Scams"

"Melodica Eruption Energy Belabored Monkeyshines"

"Flameout Headholds Salvational Disintegration Ziplock"

"Serenading Spinal Column Crumbles"

"Magic Dragster Rhythm Ass Ends Jugheads Conjures"

"Skewer Conundrum Per Mothballs Cribbed Tomfoolery"

"Spirit You Happiness"

"This Ones Called Universe"

"Loudmouth Deludes Shit Crisis Ghost"

"Masking Tape Smile At Shaving Cream Wadshot"

"Vacuum Bags Complot Vivid Hamstring Pull"

"Paper Towels Sop Violent Dress Code Ambition"

Act Eight

"Especially Remembrance Gustos Tigers Intertwines"

"Self Pleasure Progress Innovates Copious Knacks"

"Prosaic Twister Traits Data Flocks At Pants Drop"

"Chimerical Head Notes Sweet Spots Essentials"

"Horny Stride Daily Blasts Blood Mechanisms Minutes"

"Headstrong Milieu Conquers Intro Lurker Guesses"

"Strangleholds Bojangle At Institutes Mealtime Whiners"

"Crap Had Crapper Gasping"

"Dead Horse Strives Squirt Overlays Philosopher Yes Man Grammars"

"Instant Gene Lines Each Proposing Happy Face Drive Thru Trends"

"Prototype Showstoppers Unrelenting Consolations"

"Transcendent Isolations Shrapnel"

Act Nine

"Reverse Momentum Melodrama Hero Screeches Numerical Death"

"No Grasping But Slid Into Wind Bends Intermingled Blemishes"

"Clomping Damsels Loom Paraphrased Yin Yang Renditions Zesty"

"Stellar Atrocities Strutted As Seminal Compositions Discrediting Approves"

"Puffing Phenomenon Heartaches Severed Narrational Epochs"

"Cronies Recompose Tight Lipped Rush Hour Decorum"

"Cherished Rupture Follies Mainline Shorthand Correspond Echoes"

"Workweek Proverbs Diviners Flux Defrauded Rhyme Royal Bravado"

"Mud Pit Deduces Scriptable Codifications Coma Theatre Fallout"

"Doctrine Indexes Pose Readerly Poise Frigid Holograms Implode"

"Clamors Crossing Lyrics Derive Breakthrough Vernacular Nail Gun"

"As Grassroots Fuzz Memoir"

Act Ten

“Vital Codpieces Craft Milky Crucifixions”

“Eruption Sutures Hilarity”

“Energy Of Pouring Hep Cat Geysers Wistful Fondles”

“Throes Ascend Token Verges Accomplished Genres Explore”

“Declamatory Stagnation Narratives Garage Sale Spring Chicken”

“Succulent Scatological Virgin Spheres Episodic Lava Scares”

“Surrogate Cultures Fluidity Taboos Solo Kinship Double Binds”

“Counterpoint Bumbles Dimension Waltzes”

“Chastised Transpires Universalizing Hysteric Undergirds”

“For Orgiastic Inverts Register Generosity Illustrates”

“Births In Ragtime Embellishments Keyhole Demeanor Archetype”

“Suffused Mystic Pork Queens Mouthpiece Sexual Aquariums”

Act Eleven

"Overstated Hostilities Vice Grip Clusters Fake Friars Realms"

"Bootstrap Myth Erects At Brain Dials Stipulated Clicks"

"Apocalypses Resounding Pages Wave Soundless Earmarks"

"Tyrannys Sunny Buttholes Bankroll Slapstick"

"Sore Loser Paroxysms Metamorphose To Disharmony Revisions"

"Feedback Loop Repurposes Feed Bags Parallel Siphoning"

"Sky Types Coin Rubberneck Voluminous Insofar Freak"

"Whores Machetes Scars Compilation Radiates Overt Hurting"

"Subcultures Wonder Workers Crawlspace Striking Criterion"

"Lead Socked To Milk Hoary Likeness"

"Ritual Pollyanna Trucks Downy Boobs Staggers Punctuation"

"Bias Collaborative Sandblast Wheezing Eczema Out Bagwomen"

Act Twelve

"Canons Mere Mention Inflects Routes Precedents"

"Shakespeares Everywhere Doubles Retches"

"Unwitting Agents Splat Prior Daunts Makings Unmade"

"Tailormade Times Each Hadnt Braindead Deemed One Size Fits All"

"Corset Systematically Shuttles Fitness To Fears Cultures Culminate"

"Presages Fondling Fathers Antecedent Sausages"

"Lip Serving Unimpeachable Dictates Clinically Fat Mouth References"

"Extending Upending Fears Made Swallowed Flesh"

"Optional Canon Grapples Play Dues Sweating Shrines Choking Tikis"

"Upping Enrollment Asses Daddy Informs"

"Split Hairs Weight Measures Baited Breath Lineage Owes"

"Beakers Pencils Guitar Picks Slide Rules Backsides Breaks"

Act Thirteen

"Puckers Instantaneous Flesh To Silly Putty Optical Effects"

"Bread And Butter Ghosts Tenure Art Movements Rote Lesions"

"Seances Classroom Daddys Unscabbed Wound"

"Whiskers Erection Livelihood Suspends"

"Founding Fathers Fat Shoeshines Dethrone Pants About Ankles"

"Trotting Students Prop Pops Super Dupers In Quizzical Yawns"

"Pro Boning Lip Smacking Ball Coddles Frenzied Airbag Blows"

"Cooing Spitty Genuflects Penciled In Syllabi"

"Churning Altar Boys Rung Bells Atrophy Sunshines Nice Rack"

"Chiming Sources Clipping Dead Horse Whining Trough Befalls"

"Invisible Hyphen Corresponds At Wordlessly Golden Criteria"

"Opportunity Shimmers Everlasting Wounds"

Act Fourteen

"Rising At Least Gossamer Darkness"

"Throwing Plentied In Substance Casual Trappings Geometries"

"Fluidly Livous Niching Pervious"

"Spaced"

"Yielding Parameters Of Notchfit Gutwhell Reward Besides"

"Making Do"

"To Hand Run Smooth Swell Comfiting Wipe To Overall Carry Forth"

"Day To Drawfromings From Fromers From Taked Talking"

"Tossing To Side & Adjoined Accums Drifts Weave Ravelled"

"Heartedly Ass Kicked Glad To Unload Cloister Bruises In Meshings"

"Where Bloods Drained"

"Bliss Vortex Craving Inhalation Clarification"

Act Fifteen

"Extants Days Edges Clauses Configures Alive Swindles"

"Synonyms Context Self As Endless Verbs Rejiggers Cages"

"Interdicts Levelly Striking Nail Heads Intones Happy Days Spinoff"

"The Good Life Sledgehammer Swallows Whats Dished"

"Skimming Laugh Track Miscues Enrages Motives Preen"

"To Code Talking Proclivities Paragraphing Coursings Out Glands"

"To Chart To Pulled Stops To Sentences Days Lengthen"

"To Words Day Orders Torso Resides Selfs Tenets Reshape"

"Ships Out Selfsame Script Immaterial Gnostic Tandem Crapping"

"Aspects Intimacy Wagers Burned Through"

"To Skywrites For The Birds Tangible Entreats"

"Inclinations Turgid Giddy Horse Swaps Ass Bandage Sagas"

Act Sixteen

"Watermarks Emergences Sublimate Hourglass Figures"

"Huge Hearted Cages Moniker Backslaps"

"Instant Utterances Glyph Death To Dying"

"Mouths Slap & Heads Hit Meantime Fatal Derangements"

"Trips Punch Clock Shuffle Toward What Removes Natures Even Keels"

"Bonfire Toward No Expectations Safe Harbor Strunk & White Routs"

"Lotioning Notions Angels Finally Getting To Forgetting"

"Thinking Ape Charters Self Righteous Routes Liquid Lead"

"Prefaces Precipitates Writs Delves Current Events Conspire"

"Razed Skyscrapers Airline New Language Communes"

"Recharged Writhing Splays Forked Tongues Brainpans Fry"

"Encompassing Hues Particular Touts Underwing Underwriting"

Act Seventeen

"Know Where Roundabout The How Of Bombs Falling"

"Say The Falls Owned"

"The Very What Of Falls Fell By How Roundabout"

"Is No Soft Collision Leaving Unlived Words Motion Shows?"

"Motioning Disparate Glossed Aftermaths Potent To Be Obliterating"

"Bombs Facts Negative Standings Unwrote"

"Rote Which Way Bent At Wham Bam As Soon Bends Back"

"See Not To Invent"

"Taken Hunger Humbles"

"No Edges To What Flaps Lick To"

"Constructed Of Hunger Throwing Weight As Selfs Occupation"

"Where Otherwise Self Wouldnt Have To Abandon"

Act Eighteen

"Abandoned Of Hunger Self Occupies Self Dictates"

"Not Yet Confined Vast Intricacies For Choosing"

"Scant Clay Meandering Imaginings"

"Collective Explosions Birth Miracles Posturing Ore Buckets"

"Tossing Shadows Incalculable Intensities Facets In Roughs"

"Burbling Dread Down Gene Lines Pitch Black Cleft Folds Veil"

"Yawning Entreaty Where The Hell Is"

"Mandated Glimpses Waltzes Fragments Belched"

"Splatted Wildflower Hues Strangling Style Blank Pages Separate"

"Honking Swamp Water Tits Faces Fall In"

"Burbling Sequences Flow Skulls Craning For Lapses"

"Hugging Limbs Losing Outlines Parting Collations Consolations"

Act Nineteen

"Stoppings Another Face Adulterating Memory Mouth Barks"

"Amends Fabrications Blinder Recollections Paper Cut Amputations"

"Derails Hibernations Unwinding Ass Bandage Reckonings"

"Squirts Hoot Paths Wander Senses Dry Parades Signing On"

"To Singes At Empty Beer Cooler Reaches"

"Motion Façade Banners Black Arts Offhand Sordid Bird Chirps"

"To Longhand Cramps Nonchalance Masks Collective Gimp"

"Buzzing Bees Rush Hour Heroes Time Crunch Skeletons"

"Zooming Killdeers Dewy Fields Relinquishes What Obtains"

"Nouns In Nature Commodities Lesser Saints Cherish"

"Revisioned Utterings Underwriting Senses Recoils Supersedes"

"Exploded Revels Hung Huge Sensoriums Possibly Jet Plane"

Act Twenty

"Conversations Buzzing By Word Hatches Be Words Winging Re-Bitched"

"Coffee Break Trials Encapsulate Turds Falling Down Wormholes"

"As In Transit World Spins Times Forward Toward Converses"

"As Timelines Concern Illusions Constituting Smatters"

"Doing Nothing As Radical Embrace Whats Erasing Or Whats Erased"

"As Radicalized Verbals Sing Chalking Clouds Affronts"

"Wrongdoings Ship Captains Deem Stinking To Elevated Stank"

"Parading Eyes Right To High Heavens Commanded Stewing"

"Sod Making Hows Of Hours While Seeking Good Head"

"Registers Every Which Way Thrust To Sinking Hips"

"Shoptalked The Words Are Bliss"

"Slaughter Shares Dinnertime Hog"

Act Twenty-One

"Hardships Magically Holy To Ass Crack"

"Purity Hunchback Cacophony Agenda Gobsmacks"

"Watercooler Intrigue Casket Lids Smokestack"

"Silences A Wind Instrument Splatter Analysis Folios"

"Altitudes Manhandling Gains"

"Have It Be Freestanding Formed Of Waves"

"Forcing Hands To Speak Minds"

"Purring Emotes Roses Ringing Amid"

"Bubbles Is Magnificently Juices Livens"

"Blowtorched Your Loco Some Drenches"

"Chilled Carouse Chimes Buttery Juicer Musics"

"Planted Birth Jugs Plumb Bob Unplanned Hovers"

Act Twenty-Two

"Ponders Folks Apes"

"Closet Drama Mountain Blossoms"

"Stints Up Gold Days Beckons"

"Gospel According To Heap Clouds"

"Bright Occasions Linguistic Unselfishness"

"Redder Embodies Words Tornado Origins"

"Capitalized Descripts As Theories Sensations Drama"

"Authority Peaches Clowning Blood"

"Nursemaids Instabilitys Stock Responses"

"Dwindles Stingy Moonlight Appears"

"Cloudburst Criterion Novelette Downpours Physics Tracts"

"Penetrating Straddle Conserves Bulk Aesthetics Marvels"

Act Twenty-Three

"Superhighway Quatrains Once Upon Noveltys Times"

"Laptop Suicide Bomber Logs Big Chief Out"

"Composed Mimes Essentials Readers Unsound Sculpture Theater"

"Sestet Resolves Principal Forms Flowering Interplays"

"Couplet Epigrams Clowns Spondees Singsong Crusader"

"Catharsis Mishmashes Corporate Masturbation Exercise"

"Mystery Cycles Itinerant Troopers Enjambments"

"Hidebound Playhouse Bullring Upthrusts Vellum Recitative"

"Upstarts Contriving Hypothalamus Soul Food Gymnastic"

"Phrases Clauses Obliques Flesh Allowed"

"As Farewell Discourse Cloud Talks Snowflakes"

"Mystical Trend Concordance Haloes May Thud"

Act Twenty-Four

"Blueprints Multiple Rhythms Vanish Illegible Characters Scribbles"

"Monkey Cysts Headfirst Maelstrom Recomposes"

"Sodomy Decompose Typhoons Reverses"

"Grilling Kittens Forestalling Blunders Disburses"

"Gibbous Whistleblowers Conflate Deadlocks Loathes"

"Craniofacial Stationhouse Crackdowns Broomsticks"

"Charades Harmonic Catechism Glyphs Circus Dead Languages"

"Boombox Blood Relics Goofballs Speech Sounds"

"Revivals Incoming Voodoos Bouncing Tits"

"Abstraction To Fact Universes Libretto Sublimity"

"Devices Nerve Ending Syntax Blanket"

"Lexical Falters Liberations Enthralls"

Act Twenty-Five

"Infinitys Be Substantial Captions Interdictions"

"Inferring Sense Made Does"

"Thoroughbred Crapping Auction Block Melancholy"

"Unbroken Fancy Free Adheres Dancing Camera"

"Positioned As Spectacularly Sleek Head Of Candor"

"Signature Top Hat Pretext Breathing Persona"

"Wooly Atmosphere As Magical Passport"

"Propping Breezes From Narrative To Number"

"Winsome Closure Screwballs Syntactical Droll Pansy"

"Upon An Oxymoron Quotidian"

"Tweaking Epiphanies Hallucinations Tickles Ornaments"

"Theatrical Bloodstreams Tit For Tat Nonsenses"

Act Twenty-Six

"Paranoias Incantations Bulwark Monastic Bewilders"

"Graffiti Icesheet Gnaws Emissions Laments"

"Flimflams Merge Fuzzy Pants Multiple Chasms"

"Bomb Sniffing Eskimos Mime Blubbered Mushes"

"Cortex Bigwigs Heckle Scripture Gristles Latest Ape"

"Poise Clinging Freebirds Leash Blow Dryer Plunges"

"Tuning Fork Igloos False Positives Appeals"

"Crevasses Striptease At Gluttons Pelvic Macho"

"Execs Parka Vaudeville Safe Crackers Banging Gardens"

"Memorys Cuneiform Bambi Graphics To Bird Dandruff"

"Heel Commands Wind Gusts Faking Psalms"

"Sanskrit Eye Contact Cheetos Whos Zooming Who"

Act Twenty-Seven

"Thinking Cap Boogies Penal Codes Blizzards Twine"

"Rife Grazes Verb Unmuffled Nouns Gazes"

"Everyday Dreams Simple Simon To Body Count Simian"

"Folds Essences Unison Strains Apogees Chimp As"

"Ball Float To Shithead Jounces Doctored"

"Masks Thumbing Opposes As Hands On Approaches"

"Lickety Split Locutionary Freed Delicious Pinheads"

"Axed To Brambles Suffixed To Coddle Box"

"Ego Whimpers Deficit As Sideshow Terrifics Bimbos"

"Chalkboards Per Ass Scratch At Harried Mists"

"Hindsight Breathless Vowels Shape Circumspect Torpedo"

"Mental Case Shrapnels Pretenses For Recollected Yawns"

Act Twenty-Eight

"Novelty Cosmos Discloses As Diaper Transitions"

"Training Bra Ethics Commodes Overflown"

"Precedents Flower Rainwater Mimics"

"Faxed Triplicate Fictions Decree Monkeys"

"Crapshoots Uncle Innumerable Mounds For Teflon Shrine"

"Grids Deodorant Scandals Nostalgias Technique Giggles"

"Hunches Chic Splices Pulpits Syntax Fur Neurons"

"Stuffed Blood Rodents Visions Clasped Eyewitnesses"

"Consumptions Buckteeth Intoxicant Halitosis Snoots"

"Chutes Barking Howdy Dilate Blank Lungs Toys"

"Reverse Gear Slatterns Gnaw Torsion"

"Prospects Generic Gild Crises To Waning Body Part Recourses"

Act Twenty-Nine

"Drivelines Homespun Widdershins To Drained Pearly Whites"

"Lickboots Shoeshine Goosesteps Choking Preheats"

"Stale Tackle Wow Dongs Rendering Powwows"

"Furors Abalone Among All Hollows"

"Mentality Consumption Sparses Duck Soup"

"Censer Swings Rick Managements Clown Times"

"Oxygen Debts Sterling Pipes Mothballed"

"Sniper Handbrakes Surges Crackdown Steamrollers"

"Potheads Wrangle Choke Points Montages Hardballs"

"Pompoms Loose Nukes Revamp Moonwalker"

"Pages As Terrain Furthering Words"

"Ordaining Forays Delved Booked Passages"

Act Thirty

"Wending For Weights Words Through Blank Pages Amazes"

"Stitched To Dolled As A Scarecrow A Man Makes"

"All Intents The Fiction Lifes Stuffed Of"

"Coheres Big Scatters Any Scatter Can"

"Landscaping Inroads You Turn To Endless Otherwises"

"Scanned As Endless Book Grey Matter Juices Electric"

"As Sheaf Works Turning To Bound Leaves"

"Starting To Staying At Magic"

"Fence Lines Run Sentences Through Days"

"Planet Its Breathtaking Warms"

"Flooding Oxygen Simultaneously Claps Your Super Leak"

"Cheerleaders Mohair Granite Effigies"

Act Thirty-One

"Gold Oxygen Ranking Near The Top Of Favored Thoughts"

"Echoes Easily A Dozen Slower Motions Took"

"Paved To Places Times Dumbing To Swap"

"Watermelon Stint Credit Cards Levelheaded Grind"

"Granny Print Corpse Carouses To Spite Blue Dead Horse"

"Gold Oxygen Though Narrow Kisses Tranquil Puddings"

"Microcosm Adjuncts Randy Hearts Grooving Jerky Socket"

"New Dreams Calipers Miniskirts Piquant Threshing"

"Nocturne Commandeers Pesticides Handkerchief Bastards"

"Vanishing Jamming Unrolls Vanishing Clouds Jamming"

"Clouding Blur Rounding Thighs Caretake Smelters"

"Puppeteers Goose Soft Tissues Unfettering Writs"

Act Thirty-Two

"Fritters Dry Lakes Terminal Velocities"

"Sternums Thrum The Bitch Sings"

"Sheds Light Of Beefs Another Books Called Prefaces"

"Mission Statement Out The Window"

"Functioning Tits Disorders Keep Your Knees Bent"

"Spiky Collations Ramshackle Literalization Personas"

"Narrational Oracles Melancholy Tucks Jocund"

"Translated Lungs Motions Power Drill Parenthesis"

"Top Brass As Hee Hee Products Splats"

"Mindfucker Skins Autopilots Cat"

"Ringered Instant Palatial Wow"

"Effervescent Fetches"

Act Thirty-Three

"Presumptuous Tone Lengths Water Education"

"Conglomerate Pot Smokers Maxim Graduating Class"

"Ghoulishness Translates Cracker Barrel Sketches As Halcyon Lyrics"

"Corporate Havoc Logos Crucial Titular Heads Choreograph"

"Rhetorical Honeymoons Paraphrase Impasses To Presumptive Zero"

"Universe Prototypes Languages Skin Context Bippy"

"Plot Generator Sunbursts Bellyaches To Polychromatic Styrofoam"

"Objecthood Derailing Contrivances Incessant Realms"

"Collapses Stupendous Abstracted Glassine Feedback"

"Breadbasket Affidavit Stammerer Bottoms Out Leg Humps Out Honkers"

"Ditching Myths Lexical Peepshow Rebounded Hum Drumming"

"Incorporates Mystical Streaks Tarred Hopes Productivity Orgasms"

Act Thirty-Four

"Salvific Mission Statement Swings Strident Bootlicker Modulations"

"Sacred Cows Merit Toothpaste Lectures Unsayable Transcendencies"

"Microscope Mincing Words Freebases Breathing Impulses"

"Keystroke Smarting Culture Regulates Obesity Snuggles At Slow Death"

"Magical Thinking Animates Bonbons Cadavers Feed"

"Misreading Daredevil Montages As Repetitive Strain Injuries"

"Apologizes Per Capita Euphoric Opportunities Gunshots"

"Celebrations Earmarked For Culling Mouthfeel Brainstem Defuncts"

"Minimarts Nuclear Winter Personal Organizers Overflow Urinals"

"Stunting Posture Question Marks Hunches Hunkering Lip Syncs"

"Kamikaze Butt Lift Nightcaps Staunched Flows Boom Booms"

"Flows Spray Painted Commodes Personal Wagons"

SPEECHINGS

Speeching

Salvos Breathe Deranges Earnestness Honcho Foxys Backgrounds Tramps

Me

"Exceptional Jazzes Kaput Jaws Pullers Lets Cats Out

Meekness Fluffs Off Popper"

You

"Stoppers Spiritualist Iron Butterfly Festivity Meathooks

Parenthesis Iron"

Me

"Sissys Finger Artists Prick Garters Jubilance Cream Crackered Booferbox

Carnival Book Pad Hashover Boomered Chauffer Reprimand Reheats Frolics"

You

"Hasty Pudding Nabbing Cheat Animations Nail Groper Draculas Naked Dance

Superior Drag Bonemeal Observance Bumrush Chafe"

Me

"Maraud Slander Brass Ankle Contaminates

Reactionary Sully Lumpy Roar Bone Picker Lush Drum"

You

"Authentic Dog Town Beer Gut

Doing Dab Nonfictions Dogtag Soar"

Speeching

Supplementary Doink Holemonger Nobbing Superintend Filch

Me

"Chip Together Supercede Chockablock Password Exposition Brace Tavern

Anybodys Guess Apple Peeler Brainbox Alleviator All Mouth Extempore"

You

"Chumpy Fist Junction Easemen Drop Game Melting Pad Expound

Handpicked Kerfuffle Valve Indulgents Elation Nailed Ho Boots Hobbyhorses"

Me

"Martial Arts Hoagie Frail Eels Foxheads Hockshops

Dirty Great Freak Mama Eye Opener Manifest Cabooses Hummers Hung Beefs"

You

"Miraculous Eightball Candlelight Beehive Reinforcements Pineapple Kegger

Hambone Propinquity"

Me

"Junior Mashes Serious Fakement Dodge Presentiment Hard Neck

Sheers Have Dumplings On Sheers Jelly Juice Sham"

You

"Righteous Makes Faces Minimum Jello Squad

Rompworthy Pink Spiders Strong Physics Topping Man"

Speeching

Tootys At Stroke House

Me

"Quatern Of Bliss Tooth Carpenters Clockwork Orange Hacks For Skins

Lawless Bull Slinger Lizzie Up Bully Beef"

You

"Cobweb Cheat Tip Velvets Hatchet Men

Have A Banana Level Vibes Plato"

Me

"Pixillated Bumpkin Rides Plush Speckle Belly

Heads Licking Creation Mouthpieces Versing Laws Pieces"

You

"Copacetic Brass Wigs Foodstuffs Cadavers

Blowtop Hussy Hurricane Horseflesh Exaggeratedly Gallops Dandruff"

Me

"Predictively Meathound Itcher

Open Slather Meat Curtains Goofed Mayday Lippy Meadow Mayonnaise"

You

"Ram Skin Scut Works

Lucky Pierre Lubricator Putters Up"

Speeching

Spinebasher Hallelujah Hawking Lickskillet

Me

"Half Forged Hambo Finisher Dittys

Ditchward Foggy Bottom Jakes Farmers Jailbaits Fritters"

You

"Candy Ass Cannonballs Dirty Bird Grasshopper Capsule

Bump Uglys Candy Cane Bunco Squad Bum Spuds Chestnuts Blanks"

Me

"Front Parlor Cherrypop Fuckdust Great Shakes Gestapo Gone Chicken

Legshake Artist Leper Line Misbegotten Pussy Posse"

You

"Sacking Laws Watercolors Wife

Wowser Hobbes Fair Itch"

Me

"Nicknames Dog Knotted Ministration Pulps Dogpiles Palsy

Sassy Box Starvation Statue Lover Starts Shit"

You

"Highwaymen Knob Jockey Bookmakers Love Fountains

Happy Campers For Openers"

Speeching

Astronomers Blowholes Angels Tits Animal Tranqs

Me

"Ante Up Soul Doctor Fixes

Toss Gapper Tortures Medicine Man Megabucks"

You

"Gander Gut Half Cut Hairy Toffee Champion

Lush Betty Lurches Mediocre Dumb Oracle Bag O Twat Tricks"

Me

"Fists Crossbiting Cully Genitals Mexican Commercial Mental Hernia

Godsends Like Winky"

You

"Snakebite Remedy Scratch Platter Rushes Blood Pancake Deputation

Ninny Jugs Manfat Lollipop Man"

Me

"Locomotives Derivatives Kickers Ballistics

Jungle Apostatize Junkman Intricacy Glue Jigger"

You

"Hammer Jitterdoll Creamstick Moosemilk Foreskin Cone

Mopstick Morph Canyons Certifiable Breadbasket"

Speeching

Rhapsodic Squeezes Blasphemy Glumness

Me

"Jimmy Riddle Grunts Grapevine Wireless Liquid Crack Scores

Gobsmacks Brainwave Cartwheels Brainless Wonder Super Tokes"

You

"Puffless Miscellany Razzmatazz Spit Roasts Rattletrap Pastiche

Ecclesiastic Purple Helmet Nonessentials Lightweight Splatter Face Rector"

Me

"Congregation Booboos Phantasm Peaches Split Meddlesome Vicars

Rummages Rumps Spoils Puddings Brownbaggers Fuzzy Cup Chalices"

You

"Marshmallow Books Rats Exceptions Banknotes Mouseholes Bibleback

Cheeseman Reddening Backstrokes Roulette"

Me

"Chronic Tramps Sunless Receptions Ritziness To Urinate To Do Dingo

Pen & Ink Fuzzy Cup Peg Puff Recoup"

You

"Whitewash Real Jam Giggling Recluse

Cheapjack Slanders Slamtrash"

Speeching

Sleighride Slashers Play At Buttocks & Levers

Me

"Look Slippy Some Reprimand Slings Books Looking Goats

& Monkeys At Pads Of Galloping Snapshots"

You

"Smock Merchant Merry Legs Insane Champagne Painting Cat

Peepers In Mourning Languages Panhandle Slingo Chintz"

Me

"Circumlocution Rookery Geezers Dirtball Clappers Kings English

Claws Thumpers Cut Mud Dollop Donkey Show Good Giggles Don Gorgon"

You

"Worthwhile Redneck Urination Galvanizes Hitchhike To Heaven

Gandy Dancer Piss Tests Redneck Foreplays"

Me

"Armpits Piss Pipe Mouths Of Darkness Pitches Tents

Gold Splitfoot Half Goats Fabulous Squeeze Clout Sessions"

You

"Seasonals Atrophied Thighs Opener Thespian

Hangdog Whack Willy Unison Thaws"

Speeching

Paradise Strokes Leadhead Unparalleled Open Packy Mouthbreathers

Me

"Jemima Nailhead Generation Tools Dullhead Nightmares Crack Gallery

Dummo Buttwipes Ordeals Dogmatists Suffering Buzzbombs"

You

"Horse Pox Buzzer Mans Cannon Martyrdom Rear Seat Gunners Readywash

Scumsucker Masks Rotary Sprang Taintmeat"

Me

"Good Sport Blubbers Genial Geeks Collapses Carpenters Dreams

Carpet Knight Bluehair Gonzos Blowing Cheeks Blue Ribbon Cheesehead"

You

"Hurls Monkeys Neversweat Meat Puppet Rotation

Ninnyhammer Donkey Lick Glitter Gulch Shakedown"

Me

"Howitzer Samping Granny Lane House Ape Lipkisser Granny Grunts

Liquid Cosh Acquiesces Pocket Billiards Landing Pads"

You

"Splashdown Plush Sweetback Rounds Sweetmouth Spherical Sweetcheeks

Fast Track Hot Fat injection Silk Farts Groovers Schoolbooks Confabs"

Speeching

Grotto Jeeters Jayhawk Mercy Fuck Memos Sweet Nothings Dynamite

Me

"Rumpus Miraculous Brothel Creepers Pogo Nosebleeds

Horse Chips Punctures Salvation Gone Crackers"

You

"Print Mittens Barrel Shined Living Flutes Pronto

Little Shame Tongue Fort Bushy Hollowhead"

Me

"Coffin Meat Cheesecakes Skedaddles Happy Farms Brimstone Bongs

Fuzzy Lap Flounders Gadslick Futz Off"

You

"Drapery Miss Dreadnought Crumb Catcher Toothpick Brigade

Chippy Crumbo Boy Racer Blue Velvets Big Bertha"

Me

"Berserko Fancy Dans Family Disturbances Throttling Knuckles Cheeky

Ferreting Cupboard Love Face Tickets Gets Buzzes On Creamsticks"

You

"Jawbreaker Pit Holes Possum Rouse

Royal Docks Rough Trade Shit Creek Somnambulance"

Speeching

Sombitch Solitaire Minutiae Gloomy Gus Like Blazes Lace Mutton Glands

Me

“Neck Verse Poppys Toolheads Neckweed Stiffener

Old Harry Necker Rushes Business Isadora Rushlight”

You

“Jaws Iron Lung Irishmans Necktie

Ironhead Pooley Shits Bullets Tom Tart Dances Naked Skim Money”

Me

“Meccano Meow Kerblips Mega Handlebars Hand Gallops Hammy Sock

Front Attic Monkey Fruit Dodge Pompey Frisker”

You

“Dog & Pony Do Dixie

Dexters Dogs Bottoms Dibs On Cramp Words Crackskulls Members Mugs”

Me

“Moll Blood Mondo Mollys Hole Orange Banana Slabdabs

Sky Clad Skull Pussy Sky Hoot Throw A Fuck Skyjacking”

You

“Tragic Magic Threesome

Uncle Three Balls Unicorns Town Rakes Highbinder Intensifier”

Speeching

Jesus Wept Jerry Steak

Me

“Lapland Jerkwaters Lances In Rest

Lame Scene Mill Clappers Mighty Joe Young Milkshakes”

You

“Nympho Puppys Pure Love As Rough As Guts Pump Thunder

Tarantula Juice Jivetime Town Stallion Jingler Dipso Dinosaur”

Me

“Jerking Chin Music Little Plowman Pumps Bilge To Red Ruin Pig Sconce

Pikestaff Grand Bag Pigs Whisper Catherine Wheel Fattoon Catches Coppers”

You

“Fat Lip Labonza Kvetch

Mercy Buttercups Ponys Up Old Beeswing”

Me

“Real Scorcher Sprays Spectators Spots On Poon

Tango Pirate Talks Turkey Whats Jumping”

You

“Topping Mans Major Wheelies Makes Waves

Broken Arrow Brings Mud At Happy Box”

Speeching

Coast To Coast Black Sunshine Blue Barrels Aardvark Turnabouts

Me

"Brain Ticklers Abandoned Habits Battery Acid

Doublecross Mexican Jumping Bean Blackbirds Road Dope"

You

"Grape Parfait Flat Blues Pixys Sparkle Plenty Snow Pallets

Didn't Oughter Above Snake Ditty Poppers"

Me

"Cold Muffin Abigail Colloquials About The Sizes Of It

Deep Sea Turkeys Collywobbles Connecticut River Pork"

You

"Chaffing Crib In A Good Skin Above Par

Drugstore Cowboy Buckhorse Dry Bob Dryfucks Plastic Job"

Me

"Chinstrap Canting Crew Burns Shame Planted Upon The Indie

Bullfinch Buddha Sticks Buffers Nab Chocker"

You

"Dimetown Jeff Davis Kayo Jawing Tackle

Open Skather Kangaroo Droops Good Times Janes Mothers Milk"

Speeching

Geronimo Gets A Belly Fish Lips Fireworks

Me

"Ride Bitch Jawboning Moll Buzzer Muzzling Cheat

No Slouch On Yr Granny"

You

"Nose Upon Oyster Ozone Ranger Rolling Kiddy

Roger Ramjet Smash & Grab"

Me

"Apple Smellers Stunning Joe Banks

Stuffed Rat Trimmings Trick Baby Whamdanglers Trim The Buff"

You

"Trick Towel Whatchmacallit Trimmingly Whammo

Cabbage Patch Higry Pigry Chickenbrain Loddy Highland Fling"

Me

"Real Babe High Stepper Reckons Ready To Spit Highwater

Recently Struck It Ready Rocks Recap"

You

"Slum The Gorger Spray Starch

Tallywag Wigglers Talk Trash Wigged Out One Way Pockets Onionhead"

Speeching

Mindfuckers Jinks The Barbers Hammerhead Hand Gallop

Me

"Handicap Dolefuls Pervo Nurserys Icy Pop Idiot Fringe

Physics For Poets"

You

"Shock House Phoenix Rests Phone Booth Baby

Petticoat Merchant Cherry Glim Jack"

Me

"Glasshouse Lummox Glazes Donuts Planks Down Globe Joy

Steel Bottom Sleepyhead Sweet Talks Live Sausage Loaded Gun Sweetmeat"

You

"Little Smacks Living Flutes Loaded For Bear

Living Ends Little Smoke Live Rabbit Little John Little Hack Job"

Me

"Ninepins Mofo Peasouper Peral Dives Piss Elegant Peanut Roaster

Good Form Pearl Necklace Goodnight Kiss"

You

"Crocussing Gutrot Kacks Messy Buckets On Flakes On Fire

Speckled Wiper Super Honky Trailer Trashes Sushi Tacos Vex Money"

Speeching

Velveeta Mandrake Hardballs Mans Milk Dumptruck Dates

Me

“Cheese Dong Bobbles Last Waltzes Laughing Boy Oopsy Doodles

Sad Man Pees Between Two Heels”

You

“Smileys Schwag Swears Pink Lumber Sauce Clefts

Cigar Burns Chuff Boxes Charity Dames Eyelid Movies”

Me

“No Beyond Jammer Nod Cock No Diggety No Dice

Jerry Sneaks Jesus Stiff To Jersey Sides Of the Snatch Plays”

You

“Jerusalem Slim Jets Juice Hamfatter Forty Dog Electric Queen Eight Tracks

Elbow Grease Eightballs Egyptian Queens Electric Lettuce Einstein”

Me

“Hump Day Gut Check Mohair Knickers

Mods & Rockers Orchestra Stalls Pushes In Bushes”

You

“Sheilas Nick Nack Splits Differences Slabbering Bibs Skys Wipes

Weasel Tangles Beef Slumguzzling Suedeheads Jackadandy Smackos”

Speeching

Slow As A Wet Week Slap Skins Slips Sleeping A Quick Crippler

Me

"Tommy Tucker Slewfoot Sleeps In Chapters Slaters Pan
Slicing Chops Sleepwalker Sleeping Dictionary Walktalker"

You

"Crackpipe Cosmonaut Blanket Stiffs Cabmans Curse Bladderscats
Geezed Hash Monster Jimmy Galls Floozys Up Dog Dingers Flowerpots"

Me

"Demander For Glimmer Designer Reality Dinge Queens Dimple Fuckathon
Lot Lizards Number Waves Satchel Mouth Smugglings San Quentin Quail"

You

"Santa Claus Hijacks Studio Gangsta Taps Judys Tampon Braces Tall Orders
Double Shot Blew Out Wisecracks Pilot Light"

Me

"Perry Como Streakers Defenses Perpendicular Sextons Maxes Out
Quim Whiskers Pull Hemp Chimneys Smoke Malarkey"

You

"Mamas Smoky Ice Cube Hypo Drains Dragons Custard & Jelly
Gooberbrain Busts Fresh Goodman Turds Columbian Neckties Mescal"

Speeching

Jutlands Master Of Ceremonies Melts Butter For That Just Raped Look

Me

"Rhyme Slinger Retired To Stud Service Gears Serial Speedballing
Motorhead Mixmaster Narco Lunchmeat Love Custard"

You

"Lord Mayer Loses The Plots Long Shots Looking For Maidenheads
Joe Buck Goof Butts Fancy Joseph Fall Downs"

Me

"Lord Muck Deadnecks Louse Cages Honey Blunts
Livers Chop Musical Fruit No Prob Nookie Bookie"

You

"Kimo Sabe Nonny No Kerbam Nooner No Nothing Kentucky Blue
Splices The Mainbrace No Nature Kerbside Virginia"

Me

"Pioneer Of Nature Kerbstone Philosophers Horsemen Pink Elephants
One Eyes Scribe Singapore Tummys One Eighty Stroke Book"

You

"Hyatari Sparrowhawk Gear Jobs Gazelle
Slabbed & Slid Touchibg Cloth Tough As Tacker Pumped Nuts"

Speeching

Zachary Scotts Yuppie Flu Nurembergs Maw Dicker Pizza Toppings

Me

"Maunder Broth Spells Jobs Real Raspberry Jam Speechings

Sperm Burper Streaks Spider Shanks Taking Chill Pills"

You

"Ice Cream Habit Ices Tuzzymuzzy To Eyebrows

Hypogastrian Cranny Slips A Joey"

Me

"Bum Rushes Hyperdrives Whores Knickers

Pugnasty Pulls Down Shutter Open Charms Paddys Eyewater Percolates"

You

"Racehorse Charleys Payday Stakes Ramshackles Whizzes Off

Rabbit Catcher Sends For Gullivers Speak Proper Rabbit Hutch"

Me

"Spanish Worm Stabbers Raffle Coffins Rides Plush

Rick & Dick Sell Lemons Semen Demons Send Off"

You

"Tip The Traveler Uptown To Knickers Up To Tripe

Upright Grins Up the Creek Uppers & Downers Knapping Jigger"

Speeching

Pimpmobile Fussbudgets Dewbaby Cat Licker Catches On The Non Plus

Me

"Montezumas Revenge Bernies Flakes Bamsquabbled

Check You Later"

You

"Dilbert Dildo Checkerboard Dig Down

Mosquito Bites Jeebys Morning Glory Nicks In The Notch"

Me

"Piss Bones Pipers Cheeks Pissing Contests

Spieling Pisshole Bandit Sagebrushes Snob Zoning Upright Gland"

You

"Wellspring Quakers Uptight Grins Well Stacked Lemon Squeezer

Pants Rabbit Run Duchess Rum Bumpers Rum Drawers"

Me

"Spruce Bottle Coon Squall Pissers Platinum Seminary Rides Beef

Puzzle Text Qually Presh Slottys Prawnhead Rollicks"

You

"Slorch Tantrums Slobber Tootsie Roll Tops Oneself

Topping Sled Weigh Meats Wise Monkeys Light Frigate"

Speeching

Light Womans Penance Jack Weight Prawn Cocktails Offensive

Me

"Darkmans Budge Dunks Nuggets Gunkulators At Tumblers

Lumber Gaff Outers Ottomized Rubber Ducks Rush Up Frills"

You

"Ruth Buzzi Sack Drill

Seeing Double Canyons Slops Bibs Full Parleyvoo Nutter Butter"

Me

"Mountain Oyster Lard Blabber Lash Larue Twinkle Teeth

Jimmy Proctor Worrys The Dog"

You

"Hedge Docked Flash Song Flashwoman Flatbacking Drags Weed

Hard Bop Jimmy Joints Licking Match Pitch Kettled"

Me

"Rickaticks Pissy Pals Section Eight Sea Pussy

Feeling No Pain Marquis Of Marrowbones Gallows Apples"

You

"Propeller Head Marriage Gear Marrowbones

Cleavers Marbles Rah Rah To Manslaughter"

Speeching

Plumbers Toolbags Peacherino Marriage Face Penis Wrinkles

Me

"Penitentiary Highballs Crash Hot Trots Out
Kick Pad Mummer Homestone Pit Hole High Law"

You

"Jam Supper Hips At The Clinch Self Starter Hinge
Jaw Mother Jumping Happy Crack"

You

"Finishing Academy Finger Artist Fine & Dandy Gully Jumper
Fires Blanks Knockaround Finger Pie"

Me

"Rocketship Turdman Watches Yoyo Boys Vocab
Pencil Squeezes Half & Halfer Grapefruit"

Me

"Half Cracked Hairy Cup Clincher Jayhawks Mercy Seats
Panic Stations Raw Dogg Panters Raw Chaw Real Jam"

You

"Reckless Eyeballing Reads Riot Acts
Rearview Real Grit Reads The Makers Names"

Speeching

Reads The Makers Names Real Deals

Me

"Reads Tea Leaves Rush Buckler Runs Rings Around

Running Partner Run Snapper Run"

You

"Run Something Up Flagpole Rushlight

Running Range Spastic Speaks Like A Book"

Me

"Spark Plug Spasm Bans Sticker Shock

Supermarket Conversations Jolly Utters Play At Cherry Pits"

You

"Joe Strummers Jolly For Polly Jolly Tit

Smeerlaps Quodded"

Me

"Stank Ho Stands The Acid Starbolic Naked

Up The Dictionary Turboslut Tells Howdy"

You

"Teenyrockers Loose Moves

Horndogs Hornswoggled Half Seas Over"

Speeching

Numero Uno Nurses Ho Handles Loose In Rumps

Me

“Just Like Mother Makes It

Junk Buzzard In A Hobble Jumps Ship At Jump Street Indian Time”

You

“In & Out Like A Fiddlers Elbow Fetching Meddle

Fifth Point Of Contact Eighter Decatur Deep Sixes Daddy”

Me

“Funks Dairy Arrangements Entire Animal

Daisy Chain Does The Overdone Double Guts Endways”

You

“Daggle Tail Daisy Kicker Hired Gun Hilljacks Knowledge Box Moke

Monday Morning Quarterback Mollygrubs Slop Aground Stiff Rump”

Me

“Stinkeroo Shack Fever

Sewermouth Sets Tripping Spunk Bubble Hesitation Marks”

You

“Cement Citys Fond Of Meat

Knight Of The Pencil Snowbirds Stunned On Skilly Three Screws”

Speeching

Pongs Little Miss Roundheels Pointed Glass Of Steak

Me

"One Thin Dime To Rush The Kips Soul Cudgels

Jane Q Public Ass Sucks Buttermilk"

You

"Jawblock Poll Talk Rebops Slapman Johnny All Sort

Johnny Cash Moon Asses Mother Moidnight"

Me

"Psychedelic To The Bone Pudding Club Stuffs Pudding Sleeves

Giant Powder Headlamps Bower Of Bliss Head Gaskets"

You

"Recorders Nose Pineapple Chunks Head Chick Pinchers

Pole Pleaser Poodle Dink Sack Lunch Snapping Turtle Sacrament"

Me

"Wankers Doom Vibes Snailer

Wonder Star Wring Jaw Yellow Ass Right"

You

"Nelly Bligh Security Blanket Scuzzes Out Zorba

Madhatter Hypes Iceberg Slim Frogskin Cribsheet"

Speeching

Dogs Paste Crisscross Buttered Bun Jock Garden

Me

"Padlock Gangster Walls Hoggins Jockum Gagger

Joan Of Arcs Krystal Joint Leaning House Screwdrivers Porridge Holes"

You

"Second Closet Jackleg Spider Claws Hemp Stretching Foolish Powder

Chairbacker Eats Poundcake"

Me

"Brown Madam Old Trout Ripe Fruit Peter Meters Black Widows

Star Pitch Smack Freaks Rabbits Died"

You

"Thieving Hooks Mod Squad Heel Beaters Down In Dumps

Cram O Matic Crackola Jammiwham Lugholes James Bong"

Me

"Marms Poosey Naps The Winders Nancified

Pod People Plunk Down Seam Squirrels"

You

"Seeing As How Seaside Moths Tuck Up Fair Waddy

Spanners Wallflowers Grunt Horn G Strings Craphouse Rats"

Speeching

Cranky Hatch Fatty Bum Gone Overboard

Me

"Pocketful Of Rocks Headwhipper Heifer Thunder Heavers

Plunger Rides The Forehorse Smack Smooth Smile & Smirk"

You

"Quencher Over Barrels Mystery Punter Maypop Graces Before

Grabbing Irons Go West To Get Up Her Petticoat Governors Beef"

Me

"Little End Of Nothing Government Strokes

Go Wenching To Go When The Wagon Comes"

You

"Grab A Stump To Rest Yr Rump

Hellified Jughouse Long Crowns Juan Valdez Jugglers Box"

Me

"Joy Popping Kadooment Lunch Hooks Peddlars Pack Lurking Pedro

Not So Hot Dizzy Limits Mixed Ale Oration Mooner Nose Paints Redball"

You

"Screevers Screaming Gassers Roadrash Screwball

Throws Gravel Slow As Christmas"

Speeching

Talkee Talkee Houses Soft Swing Socketeers Pitch Talk Games

Me

"Taking It Easy Talking Packthread

Thumps Down Talks Cock Throwing Sixers"

You

"Ultramarine Tyrone Power Sweating Bullets Under The Hammer

Smatters Hauls Small Fortune Under Arms"

Me

"Urban Surfing Shakes Perpetual Staircases Mellow Yellow Hinterland

Melting Moments Himbo Hip Diseases Hinder Entrances"

You

"Hang Up The Spikes Hindside Of Nowhere

Cantilever Bust Brisket Cuts Belly Vengeance Bag Ladys Bellys Cheats"

Me

"Lushing Crib Milestone Inspector Milk & Homey Routes Mild Bloaters

Miller Time In A Merry Pin"

You

"Indispensables Glass Gun Globetrotters Paces The Nations

Deadbeat Bullhead Claps Bullfeathers Dead Ass Behind The Behind"

Speeching

Babe Of Grace Acid Rappers Aces High According To Hoyle

Me

"House Buddys Acid Casualty Acid House Ace Kool Aces Out

Accidentally On Purpose Dutch Blood Flummoxed Jawbation"

You

"Peeled Egg Pudding Slice & Dice Aching For A Side Of Beef

Stairway To Heaven T Bone Taxicabs Whats Jumping"

Me

"Yard Patrol On The Anxious Bench Knobsticks Knee Tremblers

Madmans Both Permanent Pugs New Jack"

You

"Needlenosed Nerd Pack Harold Lloyd Liver Disturber

Kegmegs Jigs Around Live Meat Wagon"

Me

"Gippy Tummy Gynmnasiums Gutsballs Guts Wagons

Carte Blanc Golden Handcuffs Afterboomer Catches A Buzz"

You

"Alligator Spreads Its Wings

Douchebag Drama Queens Person Of Size Chokepoints"

Speeching

Six Pack Republican Chickenhawk Blotto

Me

"Hippy Gumbo Icky Poo Easy Riders Love Bumps Moonrocks

Septic Rorty Slush Pump Fuzzword"

You

"Donkeys Breakfast Doobage Casting Couch Bullshit Artist

Acid Mung Natch Trip"

Me

"California Cornflakes Jockstrapper Paste

Pussyfoot Scooters Spunky Canyon Yodeling Wigs Out"

You

"Kowtows The Hots For Prop Art

Silver Lining Up The Kazoo"

Me

"Superstition Dead Ahead Finger Pointing Ego Massage Duck Squeezer

Electronic Cadaver Power Breakfast Box Tonsil"

You

"Doctor Feelgood Fashion Victim Frosted Mall Crawler Hondo Gnarly

Jeopardy Champion Beefcake Beats Dead Horses As The Crow Flys"

Speeching

Born Yesterday Cliff Dweller Brings Up The Rear

Me

"Duck Squeezer Gets It Together Like Nobodys Business

Large & In Charge Homeboy Holds The Phone"

You

"Hyped Lowlife Gave Miss Thang A Wedgie

Snake Check Piss Cutter Gets Small Greenhorn Twit"

Me

"Culturehound Leakhouses Dicky Diddle Gallonhead Loose Legged

Fixed Bayonet Trinkets Frick & Frack Roundhead"

You

"Stench Trenches Windward Passage Jabbernowl

Multidisciplinary Act In The Hole Gets Lucky Gone Sharking"

Me

"Black & Decker Dismo Clean Peels Kneebangers

Babe Magnet Zippers Quimbys Grommets Styling Box"

You

"Blue Hair Fashion Criminal Creepers Floppy Disks Frosted Deffest

Left Hanging Groovy Team Xeroxes Commuter Mug Slap Down"

Speeching

Sideways Doglegs Sandwich Latchkey Kids Teaser Rates

Me

"House Of Cards Dollsheets Bulldozers

Purple Dromedary Peckerwood Wampum Whips Drippers Yahoos"

You

"Cherry Reds Crashing Cheats Carrioncase

Pavement Princess Hot Squats Leafless Trees Under Pettycoating All The Way"

Me

"Giblet Pie Blanket Hornpipe Matrimonial Polka Sugarsticks

Tail Twitcher Works The Dumb Summer Cabbage"

You

"Crossback Dips Wick In Nosebag

Locoweed Squirts Among Parsley"

Me

"Worm Gut Plasters Virgin Pullets Buttered Bun Mugwump

Left Before Gospels Sewermouth Points Percy At the Porcelain"

You

"Cupcake Rhymes With Smart Cookie

Sissified Puttyhead Racing Slicks Quicksteps"

Speeching

Silo Drippings Droopy Drawers Dummy Up Sudden Death

Me

"Eternity Box Mouthbreather Blows Cover Aboveboard

Harness Bull Klepto Mince Pies Split Beaver"

You

"Outasight Lookers Fantabulous Face Fungus Droob

Chop Job Epistle Clock Dollars Butter"

Me

"Catch Wreck Hood Rat Hardcores Duke Breath

Biggums Fades Be Sprung On"

You

"Beauteous Maximus Stoked Houser Grips Fresh Dip

Syndicate High Postage Sauce Steps Off"

Me

"Home Slices Heater Sweetness Kickin Punks Frail Hoochie

Mobile Shine Hitty Full Monk Flexes Virtual"

You

"Zeke Thinks It Aint Yerp Weesh

Twists A Braid To The Curb Rid Out"

Speeching

Chain Suck Clotheslined Lawn Chair Air

Me

"Porpoising Shredder Butters Muffins Hot Wires

Party On Crocked Fake Move Eels Hips Fer Sure"

You

"Edisoned Fatsville Does Righteous Huevos Highjohn

Holy Smokes Hose Breakes Jumping Tintypes Ground Grabbers"

Me

"Licking Chops Overdose Raspy Skin Pop Roughnecks

Tag Bangers Stage Dive Swapsville Takes No Shorts"

You

"Wingding Whats Knittin Kittin Unglued Think It Aint

Wig Chop Zeroville Wooden Woman Ten Minutes Light Chops"

Me

"Taco Wagon Slam Dancing Quitsville

Radioactive Plank Riding Rattlesnakes Neckers Knob"

You

"Midnight Requisition Leopards Stripes Looseners Freak Flags

Gonesville Disgustitude Elephants Adenoids Drizzle Puss Freebies"

Speeching

Fashion Risk Drum Circles Get Real Holmes

Me

"Hair Sprayer Air Lakester Lives Long & Prospers

Moodsville Media Freak Riding Under Cover Rap Sessions Trekkie Sells Buicks"

You

"Jock Itch Grindage Double Bagger Weebles Eyes Tracks

Boom Sizzle Splash Pages Break The Fourth Wall Golden Ears"

Me

"Boofers Woodstock Outshot Beet Hearts Tot Hammocks

Spaghetti Headers Quasimodo Stoked Pipeline Hodad"

You

"Cruisin Shanks So Yesterday

Chuck It Fun & Games Flowered"

Me

"Running Lights Whats Shaking Trims Sound Tossed Nowhere

Cousin Sis Plucks Roses Girlometer Cellar Doors"

You

"Knocking Houser Bluebelly Goatmilker Grubstakes Locksmiths Daughter

Light Skirts Macaronis Night Poacher Pillow Mate"

Speeching

Rattle Bollocks Total Blowchoice Tummy Banana Trotter Waterpads

Me

"Bitch Party All Keyhole Aphrodisiacal Tennis Court Battyman

Catfish Death Gum Foot Cats Pee God Forbids Mossy Face"

You

"Screamers & Creamers Horses Nightcap Malt Above Wheat Hay Eater

Ling Grabber Knock Man Loops The Loop Begonias"

Me

"Beaver Flicks Joe College Gets Real Red Sunset Sails

Sloppy Seconds Worms In Cotton Bicycle Ride"

You

"Peter Cheater Jive Around No Shinola Cradle Custard

Possums Crapped Out Nose Lunge Shot Parade Purse Wets"

Me

"Tool Bag Starfucker Rushes The Kip Toolchecking

Pottymouth Target Practice Crabwalks Double Barreled Slingshot"

You

"Pardon The Expression Flabbergasted Over Easy Suckers List

Stepmothers Breath Tickles Smokestacks Thunder Thighs"

Speeching

Crater Face Ghost Turd Face Aches Grosses Out

Me

"Golden Coffin Garbage Time Porcupine Provisions Gray Matter

Drives Hard Bargains Prophet Of Doom Whitewash"

You

"Warts & All Gavel To Gavel Limousine Liberal Off Load

Word Of Mouth On The Back Burner Shoots The Works"

Me

"Scrog One Sandwich Short Of The Picnic

Wires Crossed Booby Hatch Septic Stick"

You

"Shitter Talks Nine Words At Once

Swallowed The Dictionary Shitstick Skin Mag"

Me

"Snot Rag Dibs To Drown The Shamrock

White Meat Climbs Three Trees With A Ladder"

You

"Alley Apples Spice Island Bobtail

Hershey Highways Something To Write Home About"

Speeching

Bring Up By Hand Central Furrows Love Apples

Me

“Conjuring Book Fanny Artfuls Where The Monkey Sleeps

Scared Fartless Crotch Pheasant Chicken Feed”

You

“Numbed Out Buys The Big One

Gospel Bird Gorilla Juice Manicure”

Me

“One & Only On A Tight Leash

Horse Opera Throws Up Toenails”

You

“Veep Twiddles Thumbs Walking Wounded

Wacky Tabbacky Walls Have Ears”

Me

“Prince Albert Puts The Pedal To The Metal

Wheres The Beef Put To Bed W/ A Shovel”

You

“Defrosted Bundle Of Nerves Burbed Out

Same Ol’ Same Ol’ Say What”

Speeching

The Day The Eagle Shits The Bedtime Story

Me

"Conniption Beeper To Beat The Band

Damn The War La Di Dah"

You

"Mister Nice Guy Fucks Someones Mind Up

Seen Better Days F Words"

Me

"Jesus Screamer Doosenwhacker Crotch Rot

Clanks Judas Priest Kweef"

You

"Pie Eyes Puts Lipstick On Piddlers Dipstick

Streeted Woof Woof Urdan Set Toddlers"

Me

"Stuck On Unreal Wrestles Cowpie Warmup

Fluids & Electrolytes Cold Steel & Sunshine"

You

"Alternative Dentition Willie Horton Dwindles

Beat To The Socks Grips Boy Scouts Soul"

Speeching

Brighty Advances Spark Burnt To A Crisp

Me

"Trip Bust Loose Five Spot

Crunchy Deity Jacksons Hep Gee"

You

"Deuce Of Haircuts Fresh Water Face

Sky Piece Beagle Ameche Birdwood"

Me

"Corridor Vamp Cheaters Floorflusher

Highjohn Fire Extinguisher Flour Lover"

You

"Grubber Flat Tire Dog Jock Dimbox

Green Apples Hope Chest Oilburner"

Me

"Punch Rustler Mad Money Kneeduster

Pillowcase Pipe Down Noodle Juice"

You

"Icy Mitt Petting Party Once In A Dirty While

Manacle Whiskbroom Wet Blanket Stilts"

Speeching

Waterproof Lulu Windsuckers Static

Me

"Rugshaking Upchuck Shutter Bus

Dead Presidents Bootstraps Intelligent Documents Grease Ape Antidote"

You

"Battery Acid Bracelets Bottoms Up Research

Doing Donuts Comfortzones Bearhugs"

Me

"Outsider Art Nightcap Fishhooks Get Alongs

Cultural Jammer Performance Panache Exodust"

You

"Bally Nipper Beergoggles Airtight Bimbo

Cellar Smeller Blushing Violet Nothing Doing"

Me

"Backgrounder Blows Popsicle Stand Weapons System

Yoked Elevator Surfing Crests Redshirt"

You

"Coast To Coast Gilligan Electronic Town Hall

Bunged Up Tweaker Rides Shotgun"

Speeching

By The Skin Of Ones Teeth Wanna Be

Me

"Biopic Drumsticks Breadbasket Husks

Gimme Some Skin"

You

"Race Norming Sugar Reports Goodfellas

Channel Surf Detox Bankable Repeat Offender"

Me

"Core Dumps Little Red Wagon Deathbelt

Wiggle Room Fuck Bunny Puffing Earnest Money"

You

"Differently Abled Preppy Puts Bible Belt On Map

Burn A Copy Toe Jam Paperweight Sound Bite"

Me

"Permahold Bone Addict Telepundit Animal Companion

Feel Hairy Work Station Animalist Ejecta"

You

"Cockhound Biocentrism Threat Tube

Desk Jockey Takes It Down A Thousand"

Speeching

Cruelty Free Stressing Soft Money Downstroke Garbage Fees

Me

"Big Crunch Thinking Mans Snowbird

Person Of Size Handholding Youre The Expert"

You

"Cyberculture Empty Nesters Boilerplate Hard Money

Handyman Special Flaming Queen Ultra Couch Potato"

Me

"Cultural Genocide Finger Wave Developing Nations Ramp Up

House Ape On A Shoestring Okey Dokes On A Head Trip"

You

"Punchline Trial Balloon Born Yesterday Barks Up Wrong Tree

Scrounge Around Breezes Into Room"

Me

"Spin Doctor Plugs Dysfunctional Like Hotcakes

New Blood rebirthing Baby Boomer Pre Woman"

You

"Motivationally Deficient Gender Illusionist Upgrades

Generously Cut Sun Belt Maintenance Hatch"

Speeching

Showing Flag Pranks Haystack Needles Speak Of Devil

Me

"Space Cadet Thumbs A Ride Ticked Off Crash & Burn

Zero Lot Line Home Vid Greasy Spoon"

You

"Dweeb Got To Hand It To Hooligan

Hand Over Fist Get Hot & Lucky"

Me

"Fifty Fifty Doublespeak Cooks Numbers Hardcore

Quick Fix Skippy Nutmegs Logroll Roadblock Braid Twists"

You

"White Elephant Crème De La Crème Gets Around Casper

Beaver Takes Nebuchadnezzar Out To Grass"

Me

"Belly Warmer Gone Stargazing Cheeses Doubleshots

Honeybunch Rides Admiral Taps"

You

"Two Wafers Short Of A Communion Ammunition Wife

Cutpurse Snakesperson Rug Munchers Gobbling"

Speeching

Tools Of Ignorance Bummers In Bounds

Me

"Cuspy Cultures Vultures Go Home In Boxes

Goes Whole Hog Windshield Tourist For Love Or Money"

You

"Baby Catcher Takes A Leak In Seventh Heaven

Fraidy Cat Irrigates Tonsils Kojaks Rollneck"

Me

"Pissers Moskered Up Like A Pox Doctors Clerk

Read It & Weep Mock Litany Men Reckon Up Ones Ream Pennys"

You

"No Dust On Nautical Miles Motherlove Montery Jack Spitroast

Rackmonster Nails Jello To A Tree"

Me

"Happy As A Clam Mouth That Says No Words

Jackleg Hobbledehoy Granite Boy Grand As Ninepence"

You

"Disclout Hairy Canary Long Bacon Bit Of Jam

Moveables Podunk Slapping Blank Tranklement"

Speeching

Washer Upper Warm As They Make Them Gun Mouth Pants

Me

"Gut Plunge On Butch Gussys in Dry Dock

Go Down The Weathers Fabulous Drop Face Cream"

You

"Cyclones Cheap Shotters Busty As A Body Louse

Boffo Acts Possum Acorn Calf Dippy"

Me

"Good Stick Dry Snap Good Evening Vicar

Hunts Anchovies Lung Warts Lunatic Sou Key Winder"

You

"Maiden Sessions Modest Quenchers Resin Scraping

Spoils Women Shapes Study On Sub Cheese"

Me

"Pifflicated Kick Stones Crying Weed

Drummerer Kabump Not On Yr Tintype Assholes Lock"

You

"Pilgrimage Salve Not Just Pretty Faces Hitchpussy

Gallon Distemper Flips For Bottlescrews Beaker Haulers"

Speeching

Deep Freezer Legless Deerstalker Smells Yr Mother

Me
"Beaksman Knead Knockwurst Aces Up Air Pudding
Criss Miss Cricket Bats Deaths Head Upon A Mopstick"
You
"Subway Alumni Dumpling Craphouse Luck For Beans
Allez Oop Bitchweed Alligator Accidental Daddy"
Me
"Liver Rounds Happy Knowers Telling Knowers Feet
Pine Box To Bedside Leaves Lids Open"
You
"Rear Admiral Personality Transplant Sidewalk Souffle
Thumper Protocol Hubcaps Dragon Chases Flea Powder"
Me
"Misers Dream Noodler Preheats Wide Receiver
Mickey Mouses Arcs Of Motion Fanny Gaps Dope Sheets"
You
"Rippin Lips Pencil Mileage Dust the Jewel Traceback
Tree Chopper Contest Pigs Skippy Strobing Stagger Takes"

Speeching

Airtime Schwag Bogart Snarfs

Me

"Drop Zone Angel Dust Kong Block Flamingo Campfire

Cheesecake Chicken Wing Twirls Huck It"

You

"Jambuster Golden Stack Sweats Action Rolling Cheese

Temp Tats Tribal Frenum Dad Bods"

Me

"Cashed Boom Sizzle Harshing Buzz Honeymoon Kits

List Lizards Mean Greenys Reaction Shot Sweetening"

You

"Nostril Shot Wallpaper Strip Shows Illustrated Radio

Hairball In Turnaround Bananas Between Brads"

Me

"Elbow Grabber Dumps Off Lovely Parting Gifts Marches Of Shame

Blood Capsule No Brainer Half Tough Loose Horse"

You

"Fizzbo Schlepper Puffing Upside Down Handyman Special

Knife O Suction Hummer Hair In The Gate Jumpcut"

Speeching

Dopesheet Shutter Trouble Funny Book Gumball Machine

Me

"Barn Burner Finger Flipper Handwashing Crimp

California Dirtbag Stripper Table Hopping Tightwads Dreams"

You

"Ambitious Card Box Act Passholes Play To The Back Of The Room

Double Nickel Crotch Rocket Diaper Wraps Chicken Lights"

Me

"Popper Rehash Mitt Camp Pickled Punks Town Clowns Water Hose Ride

Floss Wagon Alibi Agent Belly Joint Anatomical Blowoff"

You

"Squat & Gobble Behind The Stick Gummers On Scholarship

Tin Can Peekaboo Lipstick Juice Ticket Doors Whores"

Me

"Fast Knock Off The Chandelier Thunder Jug Shadow Bidder

Instant Ancestors Psychographics Dialing For Dollars Hemline Theory"

You

"Vector To Hector O Dark Thirty Ace Faces Thats A Charley

Hot Pickle Holding Hands Suckerhole Whiskey Dick Worm Burner"

Speeching

Sterile Cockpit Quiche Wagon Sniffs Asphalt

Me

"November Bravo Oil Canning Pucker Factor Soup Dragons Prang

Trundle Biff Floater Grabs The Grass Blasted Zombie"

You

"Deads The Wise Monkeys The Stroll Rips Smooth

Hardgainer Backhand Pittypat Spanker Agnew Chukker Plink"

Me

"Shronker New Orleans Dispensation Plonks Out

Handcuff Artist Has The Nuts On The Money Ball"

You

"Homocore Memes Gemstone Files Jack Chicks Otherstream

Do It Yrself Quarter Muncher Vapor Wear Twitchy"

Me

"Easter Egg Combo Cluck Cheesy Boss Dummy Flap

Ten Button Aerosmith Thing"

You

"Corkscrewing Droob Slammer G's

Cracking Out Of Turn Chicken Plucks"

Speeching

Meat Eater Hard On

Me

"Three Card Monte Multiplex Trunker Chills Convincing

Grifter Plucks Outsized Mans Chicken"

You

"Thumbsucker Ticks Tocks Hot Corners Nut Graf Grip & Grin Cutline

Powder Puff Throws Rocks In The Pit Washout"

Me

"Chicken Wing Frozen Rope In The Ditch Love Taps Grandmas Teeth

Grace Before Meat Jet Juice Gone Wenching"

You

"Dog Knotted Ewe Mutton Drop Down To Grub Trap

Flying Baker Bungo Bessy Gone Birds Nesting Jaybird"

Me

"Gone Postal Knuck Gorgonzola Macy Pants Milk Bottles

Ringworm Pocket Cabbage Hell & Scissors Numb Hands"

You

"Feet Uppermost Dullsville Chocolate Freeway Cuts Shams

Body Stuffers Build Body Packers Log Cabins"

Speeching

She Familiar Sheetrocking Rides The Water Slide

Me

"Bogarts Joints Cheerful Earful Barmans Apron Sniffs

Horsewomen Lock Assholes Locoweed Pump Dale"

You

"Sneezes In Cabbage Suck Salt Trustafarian Warm Beer

Space Cake Souse Crown Soy Pucks Sour Cudgel"

No

"Piss Parade Jackroll Jack Of The Clockhouse Mellowspeaks

Dromomania Gives Some Sugar Driving Stealth Drinky Poo"

You

"Jollop Lost Marbles Crusty Beau Busts Out W/

Breaks Pulpit Punches Breeze Doggone Finger Blasting"

Me

"Knight Of The Golden Grommet Knocks A Joe

Ghostbusting Male Mules Shake Hands W/ Abraham Lincoln"

You

"Tough Guy Knocks The Dew Off The Lily

Pease Pudding Hot Jig Jagging Hatchet Job Jag Snakes"

Speeching

Tailor Made Take A Carrot See Ning Ning Period Hitter

Me

"Whip Belly Vengeance Where Uncles Doodle Goes

Katzenjammer Pork & Bean Repentance Curls"

You

"Sit Chilly Rib Cushions Tallywags

Newt Partys Niagra Falls Miss Horner Lutes"

Me

"Lusty Lawrences Macaroni To Lengthen The Load Lackanooky

Horseshit Luck Hand Warmers Hung Loose Goulash"

You

"Gone To Noggin Staves

Feather Plucker Cunny Burrow Cherry Tops Black Sheep"

Me

"Cheesy Rider Blankety Blank

Base Crazys Angel Together Bastard Well"

You

"Another One For The Van

Lending Breath To Kill Jumbo"

Speeching

Fats Or Fems Cat Smellers Faulkners Father Jane Russells Jam Pies

Me

"Green Handshakes Heavy Lumps Gregorian Tree Hustlers

Green Goddess Goes It Baldheaded Fat Jack Of The Bone"

You

"Cause Whore Mumble Sparrow Fathers Something On Someones

Cat Pajamas Bugs Bunny Garden Engine"

Me

"Musosa De Rosa Lemon Curd Nibshit

Regular Joe Reels In Biscuits Reindeer Dusts Too Dead To Skin"

You

"Skilled Queer Belch Puts & Takes Not A Word Of The Pudding

Making Whoopee Like Winking Like Its Going Out Of Style"

Me

"Knight Of The Pisspot Kissing Crust Kisses His Ass Goodbye

Artist Hydroplug Smoking Jay"

You

"Ice Creamers Honking Grapevine Cinches

All Mops & Brooms More Wrinkles Than Inches Gramma"

Speeching

Jargonelle Oomphy Spouts Ink On the Hitch Sponge

Me

"Get W/ The Program

Limehouse Cuts Make Coffeehouses Of Womens Cunts"

You

"Major Nasty Makes The Scene Moon Away Monkey Spanks Ass On Hatbox

Northpaw Pancake Turner Like A Babys Arm Holding An Orange"

Me

"Change Mubble Fubbles Much Traveled Highway Muckety Muck

Nimgimmers Oscar Hock Pneumonia Blouse Plush Ponys"

You

"Sammy Softs Purple Ridgebacks Purest Pure

Shock Absorbers Stump Jump Glumpot Possums"

Me

"Nickel Bag Mustache Pete Leaf Freaks Mouth Thankless

Indoor Sledging Hoover Pork Hog Rubber"

You

"Keep Sheep By Moonlights Keeping Passover Potted Out

Poultice Over The Peeper"

Speeching

Shit Cake Powwow Shingle Splitting

Me

"Possible Sack Lifes Dainty Jackie Robinson Dripping Pan

Tormentor Of Catgut"

You

"Vertical Drinking Gooses Grease Girls Goosed Gazette

Goes On The Dummy Forty Fits Goose Head"

Me

"Damp Bourbon Poultice Dandyprats Dances In The Hog Trough Dandytrap

Nimble Hipped Hashover Takes Into The Woodshed"

You

"Taking Turns Through The Stubble Top Man Takes Down

Tubbys Particulars Trunkmaker Like Slinging Jelly Slinging Slang"

No

"Rubber Chicken Circuit Puts In Slings Piss Warm Sloppys Out Of Jockstrap

Skidsville Thats The Ticket"

You

"Seafood Blancmange Upper Roger Two Camels Stow Faking

Straight Trick Six & Tips Phizgigs Nine Ways From Breakfast"

Speeching

Nine Mile Nuts Never Been Kissed

Me

"New Hats New Double Six Never Happen

Holy Ghost Hot Roll & Cream"

You

"Homechop Goes W/ A Roar

Fast Talking Charlie Drop Games Dirty Daughter Discovers Her Gender"

Me

"Discount Justice Crib Course

Cutty Gun Daylights"

You

"Dickbreath Fifteen Cents

Gauge Butt Honk Jobs Good Shot Glad Bags Fiddlers Damn"

Me

"Gunterpake Heavys Kugel Apostles Manouvers

Dingbusted Hilda Handcuff Crunches Numbers Hindsight Backaways"

You

"Gladiator Schools Glad Hands Flog Dumber Brothers Gumdrops

Looseners Not Pygmalion Likely Not On Borrowing Terms"

Speeching

Same Shit Different Day

Me

"Our Lady In Straw Out Of Left Field

Skew The Dew Team Xerox Thrills & Chills Tax Break Team Cream"

You

"Tapes The Gerbil Translates The Truth

Twist Down Apace Twenty Sack Treacle Sheep"

Me

"Wee Small Hours Weekend Warrior

Ugly As A Hatful Of Asshole"

You

"Toff Shoves To Beat The Band Takes A Hosing

Pisses Out A Dozen Holes"

Me

"Spazwheels Talks Pretty Huckleberrys Over Persimmon

Holy Moses Gene Tunney Gentleman Of the Swag Holy Dorito"

You

"East Jesus Cuzzy Bro Cuts Up Old Scores

Cutware Bottoms Up Cypress Hill"

Speeching

Corpse Revivers Couch Checkers Couch Commanders Chasing Dragons

Me

"Cougar Juice Jericho

Running Range on The Hip Essence Peddles Everything Is Everything"

You

"Happy Dosser Drink W/ The Flys

Hap Harlot Hangs Up Country Jacks Tackle"

Me

"Wouldnt Piss On Them If They Were On Fire

Off The Hooks Wouldnt Kick Her Out Of Bed"

You

"Oak Towel Ocean Rambler Red Peppers

Juicy Spicy Hoot & Holler Flats & Sharps"

Me

"Dismal Jimmy Disremembers Cock Of A Different Hackle

Cockles Dismal Ditty Canal Boats Camel Toes"

You

"Cunty McCuntlips Foot In Mouth Disease

Dish Ran Away W/ The Spoon Cock Lockers Last Waltzes"

Speeching

Panama Cut Peep Freak Off Nifty Like A Brides Nightie

Me

"Lead Pill In A Cats Ass Hopped Up

Knocked Into The Middle Of Next Week"

You

"Osmosis Amoebas Motherloving Chassis By Jingo

Body Bag Chucky Black Cadillac Dolly Sisters Caution Sign"

Me

"Keith Moon Sweetheart Contract Laughing Academy Truck Jewelry

Kick Mint Sauce Pumps Gas At The Self Service Island"

You

"Shazam Schlockmeister Muhfuh Big Spit

Knee Slappers Dracula Drains Charles Dickens"

Me

"Dexy Dewskitch Shot One Lightly & One Died Quietly

Ticky Tacky Rusty Water Sponge Cake Thunderbox"

You

"Juicy Fruit Hip Hitter Mod To The Bone Hangs Tight

Grows Horns Hairy Axe Wound Fishtail Dogs Breakfast"

Speeching

Moby Dick Splits Windpipes Mohair Knickers

Me

"Cheddars Breadheads Brass Along Blow Mud

Starpitch Barking Spiders Baddest Muscle Cars"

You

"Narrow Squeak Conehead Bullyrag Cookiepusher Boogie Down

Rocky Mountain Canary Bitch Session Rise & Shine Radioland"

Me

"Ptomaine Domain Ring A Bell Reinvents The Wheel Trigger Happy

Vatican Roulette Worst Case Scenario Zowie Bumrush"

You

"Any Tom Dick Or Harry Bo Dereks Denial Weapons

Nostril Shot Middle Age Spread On The Rag"

Me

"Skunk Works Megadeath No Duh Chugalug

Body Womp Gremlins Cumshaws Hollywood Wiggle Room Showers"

You

"Power Breakfast Bomb Thrower Wows Them Bundling

Domestic Partnership Los Angelization Dear Colleague Letter"

Speeching

Weight Of The World Whispering Campaign Whole Enchilada White Lie

Me

"Weenie Wears The Pants In The Family Touch & Go Up The Creek

Strong Arm Wears Kid Gloves"

You

"Copyhold Carnal Traps The Mouth Thankless Antipodes

Book Binders Wife Grumble & Grunt Lather Makes Monosyllables"

Me

"Dumpling Depot Milky Way Cat & Kittys Water Butt Piss Tests

Chromo Dogface Hammer Classy Chassis All Tits & Teeth"

You

"Beard Jammer Fish Pond Fucky Fucky Scours Duds Quart Mania

Sam Hill Goes To Hell & Helps His Mother Make Bitch Pie"

Me

"Kid Simple Blowhard Makes No Bones Bent Cornflakes

Pawpaw Trick Shoots Tadpoles Buttonholes Whiz Mob Cosmetics"

You

"Handmucker Door Poppers Chip Dip Spook Workers Cold Readings

Boilerplate Shut Eye Blotters Paint Corners Dragging Pianos Happy Feet"

Speeching

Pepper Knocks It Stiff Spanker Gangsome

Me

"Dawn Patrol Inside The Leather Chili Dip Boomerang

Snowman On The Dance Floor Herbalizes Pull Tubes Lumber"

You

"Disco Mushers Chipmunk Music Seat Virgin Low Bush Moose

Ranchburger Over The Sofa Painting Pinchpenny Geek Parade"

Me

"Fingerpainter Groundies Maytagged Doodlebugs Sugar On Snow

Scumline Billet Tossed Salads Stalking Horses Crabmeat"

You

"Don Quixote Cul De Sac Chunkmeister Nuked Mungo

Accounted For Given Tongue Motorized Rice Fred & Ethel Cold Hit"

Me

"Chopped Fox Foamers Hydraulics Funny Freqs Weeping Willys

Wonder Coin California Special War Chest Last Supper Rocking Chair Money"

You

"Barney Fife Cues Kleenex Golden Time On Scholarship In The Weeds

Piss Freak Shellacking Honey Bucket Hoo Ha"

Speeching

Sleeper Sauce Cut Up Creepers Flaming Globes

Me

"Sharkbait Whats His Face Mob Handed Junky

Funsticks Bunch Of Fives Buttinsky Duck Shoving Cuckoo"

You

"Spam Medal Mutt & Jeff Straight Goods Lard Ass Gumps

Jockin Kickers Guitar Wear Hank"

No

"Lardo Kipe Judy Posers Hippy Witch

Psyched Lunchin Mental Loxie Leech Piece"

You

"Rack Out Dead Threads Retreading Useless Smiles

Shit List Reentry Sleaze Space Dancing Road Burn"

Me

"Grody Teamer Swoops On Trippy Thrash

Yoot Zorros Way Out Whats Buzzin Cuzzin"

You

"Positive Kill Wet Rag Tune Out Spades

Beef W/ Germsville Straight Up & Dies"

Speeching

Royal Shaft Smog In The Noggin Lighting Up The Tilt Sign

Me

"Wig Chop Makes W/ The Kings Jive

Radioactive Shack Up Electric Lips Cat Chapped Chin Music"

You

"Dimwit Supple Sauce Trooper Of The Book

Pale One Grundy Hits The Bottle Illuminations"

Me

"Viper Wig Pad Sounds The Word From The Bird

Bubblegum Crash Pad Color Head Chucks Cosmic"

You

"Establishment Flashback Groundman Grok In The Groove

California Sunshine Fucko Punch Happening Wafer"

Me

"Innerspace Bummer Travel Agent Cube Heads Pink Swirl

Truckin Uptight Zilch Vibrations Where Yr Head Is"

You

"Fungus Freak Shit Kickers Bad News Players

Bonzai Costing Clocks Asses Burly"

Speeching

Flame Out Ball Of Fire Horsefeathers Petting Skirt

Me

"Invisible Blue Honey Cooler In The Bushes Good Onions

Ginned Up Itty Hits A Flick Grounder Good Egg"

You

"Jack Up Lacing Hump Gives The Good Sign

Fall Guy Goofer Half Pint Hoodles Juicy Evers"

Me

"Mitt Me Kid Peaks & Cleans In The Ring

No Soap Knuckling Down Snooger Half Portion Yowsah"

You

"Cold Shoulder Cupcake Derail Hot Blast Prune

Girly No Bullfighter Whats Hot That's Tough"

Me

"Dynosupreme Dust Bunny Scoots Kazoo

Jack Shits Horizontal Rumble Hootchie Coothcie Gourds"

You

"Fender Bender Fairy Gags Me W/ A Spoon

Cocooning Cock Rock Bloopers Cops Feels"

Speeching

Shamus Clambrain Shat Upon Whoresucker

Me

"Squashed Yr Fathers Mustache Rasta Box

Say Uncle Tufthunter Rap Sheets"

You

"Leg Opener Heave Ho Jingjang Fallout

Tapped Out Joe Schmo White Space Cow College Dreamboat"

Me

"Beef Bayonet Fuckwit Jerkin The Gherkin Psych Out

Gruesome Twosome Freezes Out Number Crunchers Stony Bush"

You

"Straight Arrow Eye To Eye Squawk Box Winks

Wood Pussy Throws The Book At Young Blood"

Me

"Thriller Diller There Will Be Hell To Pay

Theres Nobody Home Seen Better Days"

You

"Thats The Way The Ball Bounces

Search Me Thats The Way The Cookie Crumbles"

Speeching

Feeling Groovy Gospel Bird Goes Public

Me

"Ball & Chain Barbie Doll Bangster Banana Split

Group Grope Behind The Eight Ball"

You

"Bells & Whistles Chop Shop Hows Tricks

Elephant Business Fat Show Eight Rock Fatty Bum Bum Hump Nutty"

Me

"Humbugger Knockwurst Major Nasty Knob Snot

Mouth Sugar Makes Faces Makes Mince Meat Out Of"

You

"Original Loser Mouth Worker Optical Illusions Pimpslaps

Pooned Up Queer Bashers Pose Off Needle Park Pork Swords"

Me

"No Slouch Pearly King Nerd Pack Growls At The Badger

No Soap Biter Grows Horns Running To Seed"

You

"One Stick Drum Improvisation Stepmothers Breath

Manning The Cockpit Grabber Goes W/ The Flow"

Speeching

Fart Along Gammo Fanny Rag Fang Faker

Me

"Dry Snitch Duck Shoot Duckpond Chicken Wings

Chicken Rustler Hauls Butt Hung Slack Happy Bag"

You

"Mousebrain Hangs Up Mouth Where The Soup Drips

Mouth Almighty Pump Nuts Pummels Love Truncheon"

Me

"No Shit Sherlock Norma Jean Nicotine Nosedive

Pulling Party No Sooner Calved Than Licked Amoebas Osmosis"

You

"Pianist In A Brothel P Funks Phony Jazz

Sneaking Budge Runs Bumper Kits Up Flagpoles"

Me

"Swoon Unit Been & Gone & Done It

Struck Comical Studette Pig Mouth Stud Hoss"

You

"Odd Kicks In Ones Gallop Piles On The Agony

Humpy Puppy Gook Wagon Down Home Fanny Rut"

Speeching

Downloads Floppy Gets The Shaft

Me

"Legion Of The Lost Lemon Squeezer Leg Work
Legit Nicker Bits Satans Scent Sassy Box"

You

"Bumblummux Bitch Wheels Give Cone Fat Lips
Gospel Gab Shits Bricks"

Me

"Leisure Hours Granny Dumper Bacon Sandwich
Maybelline Waste Meat & Drink Pure Pipe"

You

"Kite W/ No String High Blood Kissy Kissy
Hesitation Marks Elephant Tranquilizer Max & Relax"

Me

"Lobster Takes A Turn Thru The Stubble Locomotive Lockdown
Street Yelps Stress Case Streetcleaner Waterworks"

You

"Satchel Heavers Head Trippers Headlights
Heavens Above Heavy Soul Long Con Moon Juice"

Speeching

Mellow Drug Of America Knock Acock Lowrider

Me

"Jawsmith Hair Hopper Hairy Checkbook Half Away
Kojak Knuckleburger Ninety Day Wonder Mattress Polo"

You

"Out Of Flash Nipping Jig Out Of Mothballs Ounce Man
Over The Hill Ho Penny Stinker Peppermint Swirl Give A Shit"

Me

"Give A Perm Jerkface Man Thomas Pump Dale
Smoke Hound Smokes The White Owl Smoky Beaver"

You

"Stick & Bangers Tight Jaws Till The Last Cat Is Hung
Town Bike Tragic Magic Toy Getter Turn Dog"

Me

"Industrial Debutante Hog Killing Time Hack Hand
Forbidden Fruit Forge Mouth O Mouth Almighty"

You

"Hunt About Plays W/ The Little Man In The Boat
Soft Tummy Plugs In The Neon"

Speeching

Pleasure Merchant Be Jiggered Has A Jaw Like A Sheeps Head

Me

"Fife & Drum Fiddle Box Jammy Hell & Gone Hemlock Steak

Getting The Mohawks Fifty Cent Bag Getting The Job Done"

You

"Homegrown Gets The Wood Homebird Getting Much

Juggins Gets The Run Around Po Faced Rainbow Necker"

Me

"Rake Jakes Straps It To His Ankle

Trots Out Tools Tits Wet Goods"

You

"Writing Fool Windy Wallets Could Shit Thru The Eye Of A Needle

Pissed To The Gills Pans For White Gold"

Me

"Pancakes Could Care Less If You Ask Me

If You Cant Do The Time Dont Do The Crime"

You

"If You Cant Beat Em Join Em

If Theyre Old Enough To Bleed Theyre Old Enough To Fuck"

Speeching

Boozer Crawls Three Miles Over Broken Glass To Use Her Shit For Toothpaste

Me

"If Yr Aunt Had Balls She Would Be Yr Uncle

If You Dont Mind"

You

"Strikes The Pink Match

Preachy Preachy Screeve"

Me

"Inspector Of Manholes Two Minute Brother Twitty In Spades

Punky Broadway Matchbox Hairburger Snort Out"

You

"Hit The Ground Running Davy Crocketts Hat Check Oil

Breeder Breaks Chops Bodice Rippers Big Feelers"

Me

"Been There Done That Bull Naked Beer Street

Ball Park Figures Beer Goggles Draws The Blinds"

You

"All Languages Constant Chokers Contact Highs

Country Cousins Consults Dr Jerkoffs Flock Of Starlings"

Speeching

Glad Hand Gives Yul Brenner High Fives

Me

"Flip Off Court Cream Fornicates Poodle For Beans

Silent Beard Styling & Profiling Sings Placebo Silent Beef"

You

"Lush Trotter Since The Hogs Ate Gramma

Fairy Phonebooth Pinch Cunt Pimpmobile Slice Of Ham"

Me

"Slaves & Masters Guided Missiles Dog Dinger Cheese Cutter Dog Kickers

Brother Round Mouth Broth Of A Boy Has A Bit Of Curly Greens"

You

"Milkman Has A Grape On Milk Jugs

Velvet Orbs Joy Jelly Judy W/ The Big Booty Joy Prong"

Me

"Hot Sheet Hotel Bringdown Brings Ass To Get Ass

Brought Up By Hand Broken Arrow Black Maria Black Pepper Brain"

You

"Good Eating Diarrhea Mouth Good Voice To Beg Bacon

Live Blanket Load Of Hay Pop Tops Loaded Gun"

Speeching

Halibut Teakettle Side Hill Groom Gone Commando

Me

"Gods For Clods Go Down To The Ground God Slot

Fine As Frog Hair Finger Pie Fine As Wine"

You

"Fire Blanks Donut Hole Doobage

Crotch Oil Crudzoid Crouton Crotch Cheese"

Me

"Coconuts Can Racket Bottomless Pit Coco

Gumflapping Meth Freaks Over The Shoulder Boulder Holster"

You

"Glass Brownies Footmobile Stroke House Looseners

Papa Treetop Tall Musical Fruit Paradise Stokes"

Me

"Panic Stations Shake Down Pretty Horsebreakers

Shady Spring Prime Cut Parsley Bed Parts Of Shame"

You

"Mister Speaker Mixologist Holds The Blows Holes Of Holes

Galloping Bones Gallonhead Gallopers"

Speeching

Grapevine Cinch Kowtow Chow P Maker Boppers

Me

"Dog Behind Chemical Head Chest Plaster Castro

Catawumpus Boodylicious Coral Branch Boomer"

You

"Flying Pastry Gets It On Grasshead Flying Blind

Party Hearty Generating Place Bullheads Clap Gender Benders"

Me

"Bull Hockey Built Like A Tripod

Bombosity Ding Dongs Get More Butt Than Ashtrays"

You

"Jammer Gets Hunk W/ Hackette Boozeroo

Pneumonia Blouse Booze Hoister Cooks Cucumbers"

Me

"Haberdasher Of Nouns & Pronouns Corrals Tadpoles

Boo Ya Bore The Pants Off Bosom Friend"

You

"Goo Goo Watch Sacred Mushrooms Merry Dancers

Tax Fiddle White Mouth Slings The Words Sacraments"

Speeching

Sloppy Seconds Sex Machine Seven Up

Me

"Mummy Pussy Technicolor Yawn Multitask Mummyhead

Longhair Minds The Paint Knobknot Gone Bust"

You

"Scared Shitless Pitches A Bitch Scaredy Cat Cant Hit A Lick

Double O Double Slangs Double Quick"

Me

"Gladiator School Gives Wings Sudden Death

Three Bricks Shy Of A Load Throws In The Sponge"

You

"Slam Some Beers Talks A Blue Streak Shedded Right As Rain

Now Youre Talking No Siree Nothing Doing Nothing To Write Home About"

Me

"John Hancock Latrine Lips Fall Down & Go Boom

Everything From Soap To Nuts Come Out In The Wash"

You

"Casper Milquetoast Pounds The Books Hits The Bottle

A Cold Day In Hell"

Speeching

If You Cant Stand The Heat

Me

"If Youll Pardon The Expression

If Ive Told You Once"

You

"If Push Comes To Shove

If You Know Whats Good For You"

Me

"I Can Dig It

I Could Care Less"

You

"I Hear What Youre Saying

I Couldnt Care Less"

Me

"I Beg Yr Pardon

I Kid You Not"

You

"I Dont Give A Flying Fuck

I Am So Sure"

CONSTITUTES

Article I

Madison

Whirlwind cinches freebase commando singsong!

Hamilton

Rehabilitation maggots objective history bunk. Hurling censorship, sharecropper masticate. Whistleblower freeform, scary face swastika leeches American tubular.

Jefferson

Majordomo gizzard Marxist digital independence bombings renaissance Arawak?

Madison

Heisted goatee's annexation. Masturbation dialectics.

Hamilton

Columbus nationalism unhanded, punk radio nougat, bombsight hindsight, rethinking inferiority.

Jefferson

Sioux shrapnel menopause newspapers. Bombardment headlines Federalist sambo. Ambivalent absorb. Drumbeat rhetoric Alcatraz thinking. Housewife witches weapons while anthropologist mutilates predictability.

Madison

Genocide immersion or national interest cooking spray?

Article II

Hamilton

Napalm muffin tin expulsion, embarrassed preheat, rolling pin atrocity. Subordination reefer symposium.

Jefferson

Progressive smoldering. Patriot money.

Madison

For school massacres?

Hamilton

For cockroach pledges.

Jefferson

Mystery odor orthodoxy emits. Millennium horrors.

Madison

Kidneys cartel baby tear monopolization monsters surrender.

Hamilton

Deliberate Hopi prison publicity for dumped novel arrears, foreclosure police banking meat clash liberty at virgin steel armistice prices. Segregation bourbon preambles bonbons, mortgages more perfect union hindquarters.

Article III

Jefferson

Document butchers taxable rapacity posse to proletarian degrade, to mystical maniac almanac.

Madison

Condom sampler, dishwater porn. Buick toilet. Huffer scapegoat multitask shantytown peepshow, autonomous blame bureau.

Hamilton

Psychosis metaphors. Philosophic skylight puberty amendments.

Jefferson

Spoken words whisker beheadings as stripped scripts scroll down hooker as saliva speedway renditions, philharmonic repercussion tacos as diacritic funk, showstopper polemics.

Madison

Juggernaut goodwill joystick.

Hamilton

Government foreplay. Denouement flashback cucumber excavate.

Jefferson

Reincarnation religiosity slaughter triages trinkets, wishbone triathlon. Wrangle wiretap zephyr zygote washboards, sangria precis.

Article IV

Madison

Venereal disease prognosis supercharges earmuff brothel, anesthesia brisket abdomen announcement, chauvinist earthling passion play.

Hamilton

Orchard fatwa elegiac. Aborigine chrysanthemum deadlock.

Jefferson

Dear motherboard, do polysyllabic shuffleboard pranksters ulcerate presidencies in titular skillet?

Madison

Pitchfork motherhood. Pantomime marathon, panhandle mausoleum spigot, maverick colonization spandrel. Meteorite isthmus manhunt, roustabout straightjacket rototiller spareribs sirocco for psalm prowess.

Hamilton

Starboard piggyback, formulaic oddball chariot albumen charisma.

Jefferson

Greasepaint accelerator sonnet, migraine microfiche.

Madison

Reggae outskirts stopcock papacy. Pacifism lasagna duckbills dumbwaiter burnout.

Article V

Hamilton

Comatose galaxy propaganda vineyards trappings, terminology freehand.

Jefferson

Sycamore proboscis.

Madison

Nacho muzak leprosy gyroscope mumps.

Hamilton

Hairball diamondback pulpit rugby quiche resound.

Jefferson

Jejunum elision, peephole rotisserie, jingo graffiti infrastructure. Megaphone infighting, onomastics redneck referendum mecca.

Madison

Sketchy regurgitate. Vaseline devotion esophagus.

Hamilton

Stopwatch storyboard tranquilizer.

Jefferson

Confederate gigolo firebomb, strychnine groundswell suede stud.

Article VI

Madison

Thrombosis firebrand ungulate thriller. Unisex saddle mustache hoagie dungaree harpoon.

Hamilton

Diadem crapshoot astrolabe delusion dartboard.

Jefferson

Topiary vagina turboprop waistband voucher werewolf trophy.

Madison

Outbreaks Harlem Nasdaq, criminologist ballots mainstream perdition, redcoat psychobabble.

Hamilton

Telethon hatpin treadmill Styrofoam brimstone. Lighthouse repression, slaphappy recount underbelly. Taxonomy shibboleth tearjerker database poultice.

Jefferson

Birthmark grapevines breaststroke karaoke honorarium, puritan locution, thumbprint semaphore. Punctuation splashdowns unpublishable statutes.

Madison

Toastmaster tomahawk tonality, thalamus surmount, incumbency indoctrination. Quarterback puddings posthumous macrame. Puffball spectacle inguinal dollops expedite, pucker fatherland teamwork transgender lazybones cosponsor.

Article VII

Hamilton

Prostitution landslides urogenital layman hangdog gentrification.

Jefferson

Handlebar audit, hangman speculum.

Madison

Masquerade preface chigger preshrunk chitchat opprobrium.

Hamilton

Velodrome swagger vaudeville sushi riot girl logarithm, tampon materialism. Tumbleweed deadpan citizen fishhook brainwash. Linoleum bowlegs squeegee limericks.

Jefferson

Daiquiri lionhearted sweat meat touchstone.

Madison

Faith articles swine thruways. Musculature fricative, frolicsome daydream.

Hamilton

Noxious gnocchi novella mindset seances nuptial farrago seismically. Brushwork dogfight buckwheat lumbago, bucktooth lumberjack.

Article VIII

Jefferson

Unchristian, unattached, unbecoming, unashamed, unsullied, untested, unobliging, unanswerable, unvarying, unsubstantiated, undivided.

Madison

Untreated, unpublished, unsafe, unpaid, unpaved, unlace, unwaveringly, unedited, unholy.

Hamilton

Unenviable, unhelpful, unexposed, unperturbed, unzip, uneaten, unrecognizable, unproductive, unbeknownst, unorthodox.

Jefferson

Unadulterated, unalienable, unassuming, unartistic, uncombed, undeterred.

Madison

Unabated, undefined, undiminished, unasked, unblinking, uncommunicative, unclear, unclean.

Hamilton

Uncaring, unbolt, uncharted, unbridle, uncivil, uncanny, uncouth, undeclared, uncivilized.

Jefferson

Undigested, unbiased, unacademic, unceremonious unquenchable, unfinished, uninhabited.

Madison

Unamerican, unamerican, unamerican, unamerican, unamerican, unamerican, unamerican.

Article IX

Hamilton

Protestant pajamas protocol provisional telepathy, teenybopper teepees.

Jefferson

Xerography yarmulke underarm footrace, elephantiasis bucolic.

Madison

Stepladder speedometer, warbler thunderbolt shindig.

Hamilton

Thalidomide steeplejack trendsetter, senatorial pegboard trauma.

Jefferson

Madcap empirical gallbladder facsimile oratorio fuselage shortfall. Scoreboard screenplay retread, lamebrain fundament, pinata hubris.

Madison

Streptococcus pedagogy, pelvis noose metalanguage, Methodist gravel.

Hamilton

Extracurricular gastric daguerreotype clubfoot bruiser? Blacktop cockfight triplicate, blackout stenography travelogue encephalograph. Indecipherable treatise, incubation trapeze.

Jefferson

Fortissimo grasshopper congeries livelihood confetti, segued polyphony mutiny.

Article X

Madison

Sidewalk operetta temporization, plutocracy nomenclature, toadstools lockjaw jarring plowshare lodestone.

Hamilton

Embroil landed argot shebang, polity mush, plurality plunger scuttlebutt.

Jefferson

Tarmac subpoenas torpedo subplot, toreador pulmonary toothbrush publication, evergreen ligature manifesto.

Madison

Silverware thyroid handrail halitosis colander.

Hamilton

Broccoli codpiece apologist brouhaha, broomstick maxims.

Jefferson

Slapstick tandem skywriting. Linchpin eponym conjectures envoys.

Madison

Transmogrifies microchip Talmud midriff linkage mildew. Mortuary buddy, transducer scumbag, pinafores scribbles, screeds husbandry munchies.

Article XI

Hamilton

Lowercase tenderloin pathos is patchouli paunch resurgent, is patois skyscraper, is thermonuclear patella patriarch storyboard.

Jefferson

Pussyfoot mutagenesis. Hobbyhorse flagpole mural.

Madison

Mammography kowtow. Epigraph noncom epoxy, roundelay particleboard racketeer cincture.

Hamilton

Chickasaw cheeseburger. Epitaph lesbian episiotomy. Cheesecloth letterpress epithelium, Cherokee chessboard.

Jefferson

Wigwam gingivitis, protagonist measles. Domestic tranquilizer handcarts testosterone eggnog.

Madison

Cowcatcher spatter couscous declassify. Amendment distributor, puffy lifework.

Hamilton

Piecemeal shipwreck, picador frypan.

Jefferson

Picaresque stencil jalapeno ultrasound ukulele. Protean interbreed.

Article XII

Madison

Congregational frostbite electroshock frosting triceratops jaywalk.

Hamilton

Vasectomy tribesman, velveteen smallpox. Obloquy dogfish retrogress doomsday.

Jefferson

Tinnitus kestrel cynosure stretcher, lawmaker paramilitary layover perdition.

Madison

Dehydration pipeline quagmire bogs. Kittenish microsurgery, laundromat umpire.

Hamilton

Milady tectonics. Launchpad sturgeon mazurka. Hiroshima whisk broom.

Jefferson

Spineless meanie. Ureter melon, Sisyphean urethane.

Madison

Homegrown seasick Impressionism, greenhorn forensic.

Hamilton

Shotgun hollyhock superego uranium synecdoche strabismus curfew bumblebee antonym.

Prizefight bulimia tenterhook bicentennial teriyaki wallaby tungsten shamrock landfill waltz.

Article XIII

Jefferson

Flagship cobweb, metropolis persona apostrophe voltmeter, rumpus semicolon viscera, maypole virgule provolone, Chihuahua abacus.

Madison

Protolanguage emphysema juggernaut falsetto mockingbird garter. Hullabaloo gluten hunchback planetarium hootch lupus grapefruit landlubber.

Hamilton

Cannelloni bearskin candlepower.

Jefferson

Bedouin gigabyte molar gigolo stonewashed repatriate.

Madison

Sucrose vamoose tortoiseshell penalty torso.

Hamilton

Quadriplegia stroboscope thumbscrew waxwork wolverine. Overboard jackrabbit, overbite megabucks.

Jefferson

Conjugation jacuzzi itinerary jackass overbooks jackhammer. Outrigger afterburner adios.

Article XIV

Madison

Schooner hookworm adipose hookah ravioli stammer tachometer. Hockey systole hives glossolalia drywall glockenspiel.

Hamilton

Prodigal knickers jimmy telekinesis brownout.

Jefferson

Vainglory unwritten rump uxorial ginseng, widower zirconium, oxbow poltergeist kryptonite.

Madison

Ramadan zeppelin, honcho rhizome. Piccolo mascara jambalaya imprint.

Hamilton

Adrenaline inaction. Postmodern downsize.

Jefferson

Casino species revitalization Interferon mirage minestrone partridge shareware wellness gasoline wordsmith.

Madison

Toltec television parthenogenesis Waterloo widget. Anteater carpool Surrealism moratorium.

Hamilton

Mizzenmast Wichita, gnomic silkworm clinician pubis. Philanthropist snippers.

Article XV

Jefferson

Radioactive Shawnee matzo sacrosanct tarantula, wishbone decentralized. Debauchery safecracker saltine sanction.

Madison

Wiretapping pragmatism. Penance saguaro.

Hamilton

Beatnik acropolis fajitas jurisprudence.

Jefferson

Cancer mattress Sagittarius.

Madison

Primrose freebie. Foghorn freethinker acetylene julep scalawag sausage.

Hamilton

Neoprene ocelot schnitzel neophyte, uppercase spelunker.

Jefferson

Snooker pederasty advertisement or rectal upscale tempura remembrance?

Madison

Saddlebag workaholic ziggurat latchkey zodiac.

Article XVI

Hamilton

Snowball subscript, novena sassafras novitiate hydrangea numerology iceberg.

Jefferson

Multiracial mucus polemics, polestar meningitis. Leatherneck hyena seaweed hurrah.

Madison

Memorabilia poker oodles Pavlovian starlet propjet raja?

Hamilton

Pointillism hotcake or common defense hypertextual Mujahidin multimedia ichor screed?

Jefferson

Osteoporosis pachysandra menswear outshines legionnaire narcissism menarche.

Madison

Rutabaga slattern reanimate. Skintight Warsaw skeleton pudendum nickelodeon mastiff, fascism nexus. Chastity astronauts binge at the bestiary.

Hamilton

Beriberi jubilee asymmetry leviathan mommy tightwad.

Madison

Sepulcher thesaurus wildebeest thingamabob whomsoever Xerox yammer.

Article XVII

Jefferson

Ghetto money Y2k mosque yoyo ephemeral fart bandana cancan fiddlesticks fiasco camshaft fetches.

Madison

Canker Calvinism bisexual tinsel adagio codicil chamois addendum Yankee genie butthole trilogy.

Hamilton

Trifecta vespers webzine saffron vernacular ween.

Jefferson

Versus smelt? Nymph smithereens oarlock, fluent smite.

Madison

Flowerpot buttonhole, transubstantiation penthouse, buxom trammel.

Hamilton

Judas sag, frontal conclave concupiscence.

Jefferson

Puma compendium. Budgerigar roentgen undersigned roadster.

Madison

Puce teaspoon. Tory teleprompter, duke flaccidity, buddha budge brownstone. Diarist dregs.

Article XVIII

Hamilton

Flag flask indemnity. Indescribable pharmacopoeia, pettifog pharynx. Sir toenail satanism, Freud ravening, gratis contretemps hedgehog cylinder.

Jefferson

Thereupon Phenobarbital. Frankenstein sailboat, urbanization parchment?

Madison

Suds fez fetus. Busboy codex, baccalaureate buttocks axiom. Druid grapnel.

Hamilton

Baboon aileron. Flute agronomy. Scherzo monopolist schwa scorch.

Jefferson

Harelip freezer, stoned enuresis, parched splurge. Albatross limbo.

Madison

Naiad abattoir muumuu sherbet sped spinach trench. Jehovah, Indiana.

Hamilton

Backwards javelins braille astral molasses, counterclockwise steam.

Jefferson

Yesteryear tonsorial zazen photofinishing lily buckets Hitler, pincers copacetic.

Article IXX

Madison

Kiss heroin leisurely, recherche sloth. Sticker shock neckerchief kilocycles kiwi inhales.

Hamilton

Chicano jihad davenport, garlic predicate, marimbas teetotalling Edelweiss flukes.

Jefferson

Spock methane Oxford kamikaze chutney rollerblade aspirin dynamite stigmata goggles flyboy apartheid.

Madison

Blastoff Cortes photosynthesis trumpet statesmanship cadavers.

Hamilton

Gospel retails sleeplessness for bibliography frigate.

Jefferson

Mongolia biopsy gloss, Yemen palindrome reconnaissance hellfire globalization.

Madison

Apologist antioxidant, exchequer champagne.

Hamilton

Xerxes counterculture waterwheel legislates Topeka reincarnation.

Article XX

Jefferson

Bohemian sideburns crucifixion Sony guerillas bodhisattva bodice epoch?

Madison

Shirks Yukon consequences, zinc Zola lesion, collateral damage Torah dumpling. Ticonderoga Voltaire dropout, experimental Hindu baroque.

Hamilton

Michelangelo flippers. Broadsword anxiety ratification Yangtze battleship agglomerate, evangelical constipation avalanche.

Jefferson

Phallus fermentation? Martyrdom ideographs Wyoming margarine didactic.

Madison

Meerschaum relativity medalist concrete compassion replica.

Hamilton

Einstein rerun, piquant distortion serum.

Jefferson

Serpent expectancy Archimedes meadowlark. Electoral Hindenburg cellphone Rwanda pheromone. Batman Secretariat quartz wingspan. Bacchus, Massachusetts.

Article XXI

Madison

Apollo watermark. Minibike balladeer digestive Thebes defects, vogue.

Hamilton

Silversmithing triumphs downplays misanthropy as bloody Sunday gerrymandering, nipples copyrighting popstar monolith.

Jefferson

Kaleidoscope plagiarism, acrimonious honey texts runnels smears. Mugwump Watergate.

Madison

Unbreakable decay. Huron colostomy. Stovepipe pregnancy. Debussy palomino obstetrics.

Hamilton

Collegiate noodles ripsaw Teflon umbilical, venison wedlock, welterweight gonad fodder countermand.

Jefferson

Icicle headdress Manganese Hammurabi defloration nonferrous panda.

Madison

Castrati nickname Pythagorean odalisque, Vatican paisley Nijinsky peach myna.

Hamilton

Ammunition muskrat fairytales chemistry shrine to underworld ballerina rainclouds dissipate.

Article XXII

Jefferson

Bangkok paratrooper Beethoven fungi. Permafrost windmill rodent kimono.

Madison

Muskegon, Ethiopia. Tanguy unicycle. Postpone laughingstock popsicle lawsuit.

Hamilton

Motherwell sonata Montpelier Sanskrit Jupiter impasto, Symbolist feudalism melancholy. Chemotherapy Dixieland cheroot bronco bridesmaids Bolshevik.

Jefferson

Utopian Leningrad. Scandalmonger nanny NAACP. Mylar lothario, amputation Christ eyelet.

Madison

Polaroid tombstone, headache destiny, hailstorm haiku snapshot. Saltshaker sacerdotal. Flawless impala heatstroke, knighthood dowager formaldehyde.

Hamilton

Tortilla verso, Jungian vermouth withers. Monticello staggers. Turnip pedicure sewage spatula.

Jefferson

Riderless rupture, rubberneck historicity regress, primordial goulash, seersucker hinge. Sedative rawboned readout prone radish powerhouse, Edison bonbon.

Article XXIII

Madison

Ventriloquism duchy. Cookbook despot whips up some dictionary failure.

Hamilton

Desperado cookware, desideratum convulsion, derriere chlorophyll.

Jefferson

Chipper discord, chintz disciples.

Madison

Bestseller kibitzer whalebone dregs manic depression skirmishes chalupa.

Hamilton

Roughshod haystack junco freeway?

Jefferson

Jujitsu bunkers double clutch gargoyle.

Madison

Humanitarian gunfighter ceramics, sitcom entropy, freebooter crotch, kingfisher output.

Hamilton

Crybaby airstrikes Alabama trench mouth, kickback cornbread Spandex crevasse.

Article XXIV

Jefferson

Kleptomania quiche, Taco Bell cartography. Hubble telescope alligator cardsharp.

Madison

Magna Carta Star Wars pretzel topspin, Shylock calliope brinkmanship presto.

Hamilton

Freak calisthenics mesomorph accretion panegyric.

Jefferson

Speakeasy palimpsest panties speechless philippic, blitzkrieg oversight.

Madison

Phonic traction bodysuit trailblazer bong vertigo wiseacre.

Hamilton

Verdigris mummery witticism misdemeanor Lycra disquisition chopstick ataxia, lilliputian antihero ATM heirloom.

Jefferson

Psychedelic screwdrivers Minneapolis skulls bioethics interfaces.

Madison

Tiffany petrochemicals debeak magnolia megatrends anarchist Velcro.

Article XXV

Hamilton

Captain Kangaroo sandwiches Fonzie Corinthians.

Jefferson

Barefoot sourdough electric mower novena MBA sidecar.

Madison

Electrode proteges lobotomy sensuality lug nuts pimping hubcaps divas tailgate.

Hamilton

Connectedness triggers Ann Arbor Tagalog, frontal lobe oatmeal cabooses.

Jefferson

Clothing optional vespers upstage Bhutan barbeque.

Madison

Mohawk bearcat faux healthcare anterior Creole rock salt caveat highball mammary chatters.

Hamilton

Transcendentalism Newark phenomenology squid aggrandizement, goldfish lard.

Jefferson

Yahtzee Windex smelter evidentiary harbinger Columbine individuality, patty melt malfunction.

Article XXVI

Madison

Hypertension epaulet camcorder antiquary bleach antitrust anvil pistachio swore Whopper.

Hamilton

Blowhole headcheese rigging crouton workbench, Richter Scale readership fascia, orcas asunder.

Jefferson

Interpol pullover, surtax therapeutics, vinegar torsion.

Madison

Wombat forte corncob flugelhorn pinhead gyrate, flextime, FDR doily, JFK sparkler.

Hamilton

Bacon perspiration qwerty pigeon cinema. Doctor Kildare diagnoses Mapplethorpe songbook.

Jefferson

Existential vampirism doldrums.

Madison

Chomsky gobbles Norman Rockwell, precision tsunami cipher. Seamless Godot stomach mirror.

Hamilton

Elbowroom jaybirds road rash hyperactive ogre, Timbuktu gate crash, game over.

UNIVERSES

Verse 1

A

Universes one freedom attained.

B

It is merged cycles ripe here reaches

C

Giving up, getting splurged as one goal

D

Isolating thirst & purring perfect.

E

Taken away impressions takes away thirst.

F

An attained going out to finer notions,

G

This game of bigger specks reconciles

H

Dawning absurdities as introduces

I

Snowfalls to midnight.

J

Once upon a time

K

You're not supposed to look each other

L

In the mouths.

Verse 2

M

Melting means it is time to prop hidden

N

Behind breakdowns skulls ringing hollow

O

Celebration marking amounts creates.

P

Syntax substitutes theft as pooling

Q

Launched poppies remedy crammed

R

Clouds wetted sizzled huffs via

S

Sonic tummies unearth music

T

Recombining galaxies mew shakers

U

Twice upon rhyme

V

Stalling universes in

W

Mouths fast as enlarges.

X

Packing pleasure lessons aloof maydays.

Verse 3

Y

Remember what seawall is?

Z

Puts triggers on high tides

A

After voices play for open eyes.

B

Puffed innovative screws attitudes out loud,

C

Self-pleasure popping off.

D

As foggy sonnets headnotes target.

E

Cessation repairs chronic articulation

F

Ranges as essential blasts glottal

G

Taps on smokestacks.

H

Are waves & nipples swerving nucleus

I

Only acts to injure blamed fetches?

J

Baubles convictions at last impresses.

Verse 4

K

Combining sounds, growing rules

L

To rubrics or rocks asunder,

M

Mapping arrivals

N

Chicken did once hover.

O

Fattened hasps as resultant lurching at

P

Edges as sentences fake own tones

Q

As crotches in silence twice-over confirm

R

Thundering lengthways

S

Trouble born of water.

T

Seals blots, renews hoarfrost volcano napes

U

Reversed pudding bushes providence shushed

V

Strengthening rapidly despite precision taints

Verse 5

W

Orchards sank alleluias paragraphs drake.

X

Casketing befriends miniscule icebergs, steams

Y

Extraordinary antlers episode humming books

Z

Aground, almost like vulva collapses elk.

A

Monolith defacements from blessed wishing

B

Midwinter napkins quake right contours jogs

C

Unreliably. Ropes prince pines shaggy, hatch

D

Indulgenced seafloor fees, awls leafing

E

Surfaces. Every single thing a lovely curtain, golden

F

Hinds, antibodies frequently swimming. Heads

G

Numb nuts premium recompense squats. Liberating

H

Choppers, carefree might be screwballs.

Verse 6

I

Underwent chic, yet diminution as deliverance reveals

J

Blind control, slaphappy & peppy sifting

K

Wellsprings collective elicits. Censors gazes relative

L

Lyrics landfall fuckers

M

Artistic streaks, underwear steaks, unfit

N

Declinations bungees humps conventions

O

Last legs, drifting correlations vipers whisper

P

Elation dear hearts only fleshy parts. Recomposes

Q

Swerves seaming some buckling & hallucinating

R

Revisions freshens disco, rancorous dancers

S

Blowing delight, purring countdown. Underfoot

T

Wombs defective flags plowshares candy.

Verse 7

U

Repairmen truce cookie supervision, hummingbirds

V

Propensity mangroves depending uvulas teaspoons

W

Grammars punctuations, grapefruits handwringing

X

Eyelets kingdoms leak crowned accident leagues, spawn

Y

Mastodon, Massachusetts. Dimples glow

Z

Raggedy cancer, mantis electric beans. Containment

A

Rooks tarantula classic handles, tricky tempers

B

Waylays sounds footsteps take unsteady aim. Ditches

C

Corsets reactive sheets, steps toward epilogues enslaved

D

That heads might someday be metallic. Aortas, toward the

E

Beginning of a dream, cashflow cartoon iterations to upper

F

Adores all them scrapbook memories bosoms glaze.

Verse 8

G

Rebooting more propositions hinging than

H

Braless cows endow, heavy freedom beefs

I

Plainsong jelly amasses, disintegrates imperatives

J

Toothache interpretive umbrellas ventriloquists

K

Whitecap. Graffiti velvets pedigree sighs, valor

L

Throbbing handcuff to frowned merriment

M

Vestiges fly. Postscript litterbug retches hatchways as

N

Handlebar revivals steamships lisp. Amygdala masterpiece

O

Ambulance chowder mousetraps manatee pushover, jug

P

Aliments, pretty about ghoul. Pranks juniper liver

Q

Preschool, astronaut sugar, thesaurus puppet thickets

R

Thermal law goat theorizes. Loin macron

S

Flowers loll, sumac wheel pocketknife romp.

Verse 9

T

Spleen decals glockenspiel flipper, hyena past

U

Hydrogen lathe. Batter phonics. Art bombing theft

V

Sermons smelly lover, antonym gearwheel

W

Transplants speech gauntlets as duck illnesses

X

Tunneling darling database courageous

Y

Cartwheels demark. Saltwater moonlight, keepsake

Z

Bullfrog, buckwheat amidships. Election

A

Joystick. Hemlock jukebox deeds larynx hooves

B

Language dewlap clues muzzling, ownership

C

Porridge. Vascular taboo granite elf pastry

D

Longitudinal. Spit knockers. Might missed were

E

Ago. From the neon attack the thrill water will

F

Ripple. Hopper interjection, major book minuet.

Verse 10

G

Ironed children landlocked horsepower, practically.

H

Hourglass rivalry. Celery puck goalkeeper yawn. Chuckling

I

Recon just the one universe maintains, deft syringe

J

Entertaining pillow. Proper tugboat tattoos charity piers.

K

Rawhide semicircle slot broth. Seasoning ashamed urchins

L

Propeller odds prom, Missouri skim pregnancy skewer.

M

Postmark mummy. Lovebird jubilee, counterclockwise

N

Backfires abacus musket. Leopard opera, lumberjack

O

Mumps. Soapsuds couch slingshot juice porthole, sapphire

P

Mustache. Dinosaur chipmunk carburetor Mauritania

Q

Fuzz. Blackmail wheezes qualms, planetarium ostrich

R

Printouts. Accommodating horror, aspirational homophone

S

For humankind gelding billets dreaming mounting shockproof unity.

Verse 11

T

Ambition belays prone humus palaces yell as

U

Hairless aurora coagulates recurrence. Adamant

V

Havoc the corpuscle book. Headlong halves dangle

W

Fatherlands valves. Dismays suet, felonious

X

Lather, squat worry honey cheat. Knowledge personnel

Y

Titmouse exhilarated. Ostracism listlessness all except

Z

Nightfall. Pus crown. Dear molder, postpone

A

Closure. Surroundings acids. Metropolitan turkey

B

Microscope fritters geophysics waters rage frontiers

C

Made squirrels add eyelashes. Dew chortle unison

D

Chute. Pallor eats poverty melody remakes puberty

E

Opera. Oceans crib casserole phrases, pickerels howling

F

Buckskin surfboards vassals dream.

Verse 12

G

Tailspin phonics earshot depositions for parenthetical

H

Cud, joust amount swinging menstruation pickaxe, knothole

I

Commotion summarizing pulp, tempo liveried, joystick

J

Confessional, tamale physique. Kitty hums freckles

K

Adverbial, haunches frisking longhorn

L

Powwow croquette rapidly nutshells.

M

Sissy ramrod implores coconut teens to properly

N

Shrill cabbages. Harpoons swap nylon technology

O

Sonar clucks praise spry sanity unhitches

P

Utah waistband hawking numberless

Q

Lynching, tractor dendrite poppy enriching deputized

R

Vim. Lesion mulch. Hopi internet schoolgirls waffles.

Verse 13

S

Vapid sentences taxpayers skunk bloom

T

A clods allotment skyscraper bondage, roadrunner

U

Maracas. Curfew banner manholes circumlocution

V

Cumulous slobbers. Merges nuthatch linoleum, cycles

W

Right here, grounding mastodons that once hovered.

X

Anemone bedspread, ocelot cunnilingus. Numerical

Y

Vomit, counting down, shatters endpoints

Z

Disfigurement must, minus lipstick, narrate as fuselage

A

Placekicks bighorns prodigal. Jalopy turtledoves prosaic

B

Scurf, litmus geyser hen knuckling gigabyte vampire to

C

Slattern bagpipes. Skylark foible games popcorn

D

Unicorn pins down polyglot while quail reverses ingot.

Verse 14

E

Reincarnation dustpan. Octopus lob. Sternum jelly.

G

Wingspan cruller. Viola endocrine. Gibbon

H

Honeycombs songbird integers, hostility

I

Pelvis blunderbuss gubernatorial scuff phobia

J

Cinnamon espionage. Rejoice soot dungs

K

Ourselves. Fetus workbench. Lordship cactus

L

Endpoints dimples gallows snicker. Commode

M

Regattas makeshift fat rippling cowbird to

N

Timberline wisdom riff. Tightwad waltzes jawbones

O

Cowgirls blowtorch, floodwaters brindled. Minnesota

P

Tweezers Vireo offshoot. Pollination turtleneck, plover

Q

Shellac. Viscountess thresher, sledgehammer outshine.

Verse 15

R

Eyeball funnel searchlights werewolf vanilla as

S

Grenadine crosscut maw, kickstand moss thence

T

Stiffening Algerian crater spices popping jackrabbit

U

Ice sonnets to motorboat lung stew, seedpod

V

Rebate, bonnet palpitate. Petroleum ladyship tabernacle

W

Venison whirr. Gabardine crossbow thaw, weed

X

Sedan. Gemini welters. Stingray rumbles backflow

Y

Chitlin saliva hydrant parachutes. Afterimages are elsewhere.

Z

Popular trachea saints sailboats, cow providence, misery

A

Heaven. Mood scheme reigns winging cerebrum mannered

B

Brandy nerves. Chlorophyll reimbursement. Oversleep sword institute

C

Purrs adverbials aristocrat spacewalk soundboard topples.

Verse 16

D

Whorehouse stopwatch, rigatoni calliope. Enchilada

E

Wildfire, mortuary gangplank thermometer. Groundswell

F

Phonebook, cavalcade whippet, boomerangs appendages

G

Heroically, accidental testicles, pistachio goiter

H

Sinsemilla. Loser quacks orgasm, inky muffler

I

Stings, rancid blimp karma. Bordello marshmallow spanks

J

Urinal quits, underground punk reaches, crafting bedazzled

K

Replies. Friends whoosh libraries. Thanks, obsession. Skateboarder

L

Sickness muffles naughty blitzkrieg homeboy knuckles

M

Port holes butterscotch. Graveyard discography bullwhip

N

Creeds, crackpot blockbuster tap dance, friendship pelican

O

Askance. Platypus storyline, bumblebee midshipman gravy.

Verse 17

P

Baptismal whisker coronation, snake saddle, synthesis

Q

Chalice, labial bobolink. Entropic dismissal, subculture

R

Astrolabe. Coaxial nosebleed clutters ethics tonic

S

Ethos rebus, tonal bathos thesis, bigmouth adventure

T

Feces. Autopsy dreamscapes, sausages namesakes. Chickadee

U

Velocipede. Institutionalized ptomaine dipstick namedrops

V

Accordion starship powder horn, greenback

W

Devotional. Dismember what seizures are. Once upon

X

A time, snowfalls to midnight, absurdities dawning as introduces

Y

Speak bigger reconciles, taken away impressions taking away

Z

Thirst, purring perfect, giving it up, splurged as one goal, as merged

A

Cycles ripe here reaching universe as one freedom attained.

SAYS

ACT 1

Her Clarity Dazzles Us

Rigorous Versus Rigor Mortis, A Living Saint Because Of This. Ninety Seconds To Midnight, Just Now Starting To Suck Out Loud. Fusspot Attacks Fuzzballs, Then Broomsticks Contact Shins. Some Moments Are Almost Miraculous. Doing That, You Can Dial What The Sky Should Look Like. If This Robot Cannot Human Then What Is It Innocent Of?

The Painting Of Ideas

Do You Remember Motherfucker? Clavicle Outreaches Xenon Waddle While Curvature Teaches Cling Peaches. A Snapping Turtle Waffle Iron And A Cosmography Watershed Dumbfounded. Oh And Reprehensible Spunks Midget Sprinkling, And Cows Peel Instant Medley. Bouffant You Too Much, As Coquettish Would Dick Her Fault.

Count Them On One Hand

Trysts Feign Blankets to Shreds, And Dirty Seems To Be Our Walkabout Scales. Plays Dumb, Vintage Money Brushes, Honey Are No Extra Pig. Persuading Her Frizzy Carcass Haphazard, Throbbed Nightgown Knocks Charades, Filth A Pile Of Loud Enough Thongs. For The Decorated Hooker There's No Difference Between Eternity And Anything At All.

Candy Glands

Trampled By Ellipsis, Convergence By Fumble, Typhoon Baggie Laundromats Ministry To Textbooks Ripples, Huffing Conga Into Cosmos, Fishhook Nipples Creeping Underscore As Though Flinching Wishes Sugar Conveyances For Psychopath, Adrenal Gland Bitters Sausages Clutter, Astrolabe Tedium Puckering The Yawned Colors Like Rancid Butter.

Act 2

Maelstrom Squeeze

Hadn't Panties Eventually Undulate Reproofs of Continuity, Poofs Of Calamity? Evensong Photosphere Hoots And Hollers Checkerboard Photogravure Stipple As Vichyssoise Weevil Melancholia, Untold Creases Neuter Cowgirl's Pigtails Dangling In Soup, Glossolalia Smearing Duck Lips Quacking Chased Oofs, Ventriloquism Octopi As Bridesmaid's Expletives.

Wheelbarrow Like A Wave

Cinderblock Eggplant And Wordless Honey Bun Rupture Sequin Something Urgent, Fake Gentian To Ruby Brute Fruit, Spunky Goliath Hacking Cred, Cockles To Vertex, Thinkers To Fevers. Foggy Prevarications Bend Ear At Headless Mannequin Ballads, Signed-On All Grizzled And Limp-Wristed So That Hyperbolic Might Be Fixed To Oppression's Chimes.

Lemons A Flawed Human

To Ragamuffin Radioactivity, To Inductee Masquerade Inertia, To Mastodon Call And Response, Zero Eyes And Pursed Lips Pout Fixity In Gold Leaf. Sure, Chest Of Drawers Had Firmed Her Smile. I Thought I Had No More Rock, And You Have Some Kind Of Secret Motor Inside You Announcing It's An Overlapping Microcosm Of Burst Languages, A Silent Tongue Engine.

Separation Becomes Complete When The Breathing Stops

Causing Earthquakes, As Necks Will Attest, Like The White Tuck And Roll Casket We're Fantasizing, Isn't Causing Purring. We Can't See The Box. The Box Of Chaos Moved Outside Where We Can't Prove Where The Box Is. Will intertwine A Kind Of Lack Of Anything Graspable, The Visible Tangled To Where It's Just Doom Left, The Hands And Feet Becoming Purplish.

Act 3

Tell Me How This Ends

Famous And Compact, A Giant Squid Been Big On Focus, On Passions Called Chimeras. Sometimes There Is A Surge Of Beauty. A Thirst Trap Debris Field Stumbling Tragedy's Shape While Tremendously Answering Telephones, Narcos Into The Blades, Scuba Some Sort Of Madness. Lisp When Using These Proofs, Skin Plugs Speaking In Tongues And With Kisses.

Deterioration Type

She Herself Had Hoped To Find Just The Right Texts Daylight Confers As Cadences Since Indexical Bundles Of Depicts And Drawn Marks Seeding Surfaces Are But Tenderness To Underwrite Tornado's Tinctured Icons Choreographed Cryptic As Habitual Overdosing. Hey, Let's Snafu Pillowcases Of House Martins Into Supine And Marvelous Mufflers.

The Confines Of Literature

Considering All That Might Be Said To Be Invested In The Leakiness, Super Volcano Says Invisibility Is The Web Of Competing While Fingered Behind The Cotton Gin, Unmarked Graves Purporting Plenty Of Guidance, Fatal Father's Flaw His Fatal Fall. The Hungry Gut Of The Other Day Is Today's Gut, Presuming Guilt, Premise Cawed, Flesh Crawled.

Bricolage Of Modes

As Feisty Lay Dying, Historical Trauma Considers A Baby Buggy Upended By The Tragedy Of History, Disrupted By Constant Awareness And Held Together By Stars Only To Be Disassembled And Then Forgotten, Cut By A Whip, To Be A Convict's Badge Thrown Into The Unknown. The Audience Responds Enthusiastically To Her Flashing Her Chest As Concerns Eclipses.

Act 4

A Lie Detector The Size Of The Galaxy

Hollow Gods Mean Ease And Balance As Clay Into Shapes Aims To Formulate Never Quite A Reconciliation. Ill Affording Ambiguity, Triggers Process Water Nymphs Immediately Bemoaning A Broader Flagship. Brushstrokes Of Found Images Document Creamy Impassiveness, Dwell Upon Discomfort Reclined In Anguish, Floating, Manipulated And Disinfected.

Disfigurations

Freely Drawn Swirls, And You With All Your Ribcages, Are A Celebration Of Arbitrariness To Manifest Some Apparent Chaos. Any Further Thinking Will Need To Emerge From And Circle Back, Cleverly Pointing The Viewer's Eye To Repurposed Aesthetics. The Frame Marks The Frontier Shot Through With Desire, Pure And Revolutionary Play.

Disconfirmations

Due To Your Insistent Aura Belonging To A Form Of Organizational Storytelling, I Thought You Were Talking About Bitch Chicken. Just Feed Me. Don't Force Me To Make Any Decisions. No Pattern-Seeking And No Meaning-Making. Living And Telling Might Be Different Things. Might Be Evolution By Jerks, No Conversations In The Trash. Making The Road By Walking It.

Something Of A Low Point

A Dazzling Meteor No Sooner Seen Than Gone, A Brothel Comparison Rattling Wishbones To Mumbles Limpid And Vanquished, A Queasy Defeating, A Falling Tree Falling, A Blind Eye Seeing. A Club-Footed Dancer Mounting Ham, A Species Of Rugged Individualism So Fecund As To Be Defenseless Against Handkerchief Trepidations.

Act 5

Mawkish Semaphore Jerked His Thumb

Covet Then Crisscross Then Time Itself Becomes An Event. Clavicles Cement Comets, Cramming Corps And Clawing Chromatically, Shapeshift Fairy Tales Into Braille. Sublime Becomes Pastiche, Symbolism Takes Up Slack, No Other Earthly Sensation More Tawdry Than Differentiating Between Emotions And Happy Endings, Magic Radiating Greased Poetries.

Sound Of Pleasure Trophies

Porn Props Pleasant Entanglement Themes Per Cloaked Templates Metastasizing Leopards, Couching Nuances Swallowed And Wayfaring Brutality, A Collaborative Suffering Of Already Lacking, As Much As Vanishing Reverie Is Pomp Enough, As Though Freedom Of Peach Were An Enormous Extremity, And Jurisprudence A Blowjob Brighter Than The Sun.

Public Knowledge Stuck At A Metaphor

Cheesy Litmus Gainsays An Ephemeral Erection Powered By Some Eternal Deflections Worrying Nothingness' Stalled Default, Cozy Annihilation While Sickbed Haystack Undulates Reading Distances Lab Rats Scurry, Freak's Wasteland A Communal Tattoo Toward Nakedness, Pratfalls Overpowering Jubilation Mispronouncing Pattycake Too Swollenly.

Clung To Imagination A Great Hammer

Hammering's What Binds Any Limbo, Is What Blames A Ghetto, Double-Bound And Jumbo From The Get-Go. Isolation Inversely Flattening Dazzling Antiquities' Patinas While Personae Tapestry Their Own Sonnets Is Dimensionless Underwater Oxygen Integration, Impediments To Communication, Largesse Realms Freaking Dancing Faces' Disguises.

www.ingramcontent.com/pod-product-compliance
Lightning Source LLC
Chambersburg PA
CBHW080449170426
43196CB00016B/2731
9781948637107